The **POWER** Series

SWAT TEAM

Police Special Weapons and Tactics

Hans Halberstadt

Motorbooks International
Publishers & Wholesalers

Dedication
To my two young nephews,
Francis Joseph Horton and Brian Joseph Ensor,
both rowdy young lads who constitute
our own family SWAT team.

First published in 1994 by Motorbooks International Publishers & Wholesalers, P.O. Box 2, 729 Prospect Avenue, Osceola, WI 54020 USA

© Hans Halberstadt, 1994

Motorbooks International books are also available at discounts in bulk quantity for industrial or sales-promotional use. For details write to Special Sales Manager at the Publisher's address

Library of Congress Cataloging-in-Publication Data

Halberstadt, Hans.
   SWAT team/Hans Halberstadt.
      p. cm. —(The Power series)
   ISBN 0-87938-877-3
   1. Police—Special weapons and tactics units.
   2. Police—United States—Special weapons and tactics units. I. Title. II. Series: Power series (Osceola, Wis.)
   HV8080.S64H35   1994
   363.2'32—dc20   94-1684

On the front cover: A SWAT Team, about to make their dramatic entrance.

On the frontispiece page: This officer carries an H&K MP-5 in the approved manner for the range or on an op: finger out of the trigger guard until ready to fire, muzzle always in a safe direction. There are no accidental discharges in police work, only negligent ones.

On the title page: On the other side of those boxes is the bad guy. The entry team has moved to this final assault position within a warehouse, their last cover and concealment position. The advance to this position has been virtually silent. But now it will become quite noisy as stun grenades detonate.

On the back cover: Top, the Modesto (California) Police Department SWAT Team. Below, a SWAT Team member with his Heckler & Koch MP-5.

Printed and bound in Hong Kong

Contents

Acknowledgments

I'm particularly indebted to my extraordinary friend and associate, Dr. Ron Martinelli, for much assistance and insight. Ron has all the savvy of a beat cop, combined with the academic training and experience that provides an unusually wide perspective. Ron's extensive study of the dynamics of violent offenders, officer survival, and the tactical use of defensive force makes him one of the best law enforcement trainers in the United States. As a recognized trainer of SWAT teams and a veteran of sixteen years of high-risk assignments with the San Jose (California) Police Department, Ron has brought a special set of insights to this project.

The Reno (Nevada) SWAT team was exceptionally generous with their support, thanks in part to the department's superb and admired chief, Richard Kirkland. This small team has a training program and a set of performance standards that are higher than many of the elite units I've worked with in the past. After watching them train for a while I had no qualms accepting Sgt. Steve Pitts' invitation to sit "in the chair," as they call it, a training exercise where the team members shoot past people, who are role-playing hostages, at small targets on the walls of a small room. This kind of intense, potentially dangerous training is exactly what the military ought to do—but doesn't. It is the kind of training that produces a superbly adept team of men and women who are rated among the best of all teams in the nation, regardless of size.

Thanks also to the SERT unit from the Modesto (California) Police Department, another excellent team that supported this book. My combat pistol technique was given a huge boost after a session with Officers Vince Bizinni and Dave Sundy. Thanks also to Lt. Ron Sale and Sgt. Mike Zahr for their help, and particularly to Det. Jon Hans Buehler for his help with the shooting skills portion of the text. The Modesto and Reno departments prove how much a small department, with limited resources, can do with intelligent people and good leadership.

Preface

The dilemma for a project like this, where life and death issues are involved and where the information presented could compromise operations and endanger people, is to decide how much to tell and how much to omit. We had to assume that this book, like my books about the Green Berets and SEALs, will fall into the hands of the opposing team, and therefore we had to be very careful about its contents. You don't see a lot of books detailing how SWAT teams conduct business for these reasons. Unlike some other authors whose commitment is to the story, our commitment first and foremost is to the community we describe. It was a privilege and a pleasure to watch the SWAT teams of several communities train and operate—and that was the result of a certain amount of trust, a trust that must be honored.

You also don't see a lot of books about SWAT team operations because members of all information media, including book authors, are generally regarded as unethical and treacherous. But the Motorbooks Power Series of books has set a high standard by presenting intimate looks into exotic military communities like the Green Berets, designed to respect their security needs.

We have left out certain details that a criminal might use to defeat an operation or an operator, yet have provided a generally detailed and entirely accurate view of the SWAT mission. And the manuscript has been reviewed by each of the departments that cooperated, just to make sure they are comfortable with the level of "exposure."

If you are really interested in the finer points of the art, and happen to be a law enforcement professional, there are many classes available from private and public agencies. Among these, I am happy to recommend:

Martinelli & Associates: Justice Consultants, Inc., Dr. Ron Martinelli, Director
P.O. Box 6255, Los Osos, CA 93402-2710
Phone (805) 528-3518. ASLET member
Gunsite, P.O. Box 401, Paulden, AZ 86334
(602) 636-4564
Heckler & Koch Training Division
21480 Pacific Blvd., Sterling, VA 20166
(703) 450-1900

I'm also happy to recommend the following custom maker of assault vests and related equipment. These folks supply, among others, the US Navy SEALs—and they make good stuff.

Blackhawk Industries, attn.: Mike Noell
2413 Bowland Pkwy #102,
Virginia Beach,
VA 23453
(804) 486-8254

Chapter 1

Introduction

We were pressed up against the side of a dirty and dilapidated old house, ready to serve an arrest warrant, endorsed for night service, on a short, fat, nasty little guy whose name I've forgotten. It was very early in the morning, about 0430 hours, a time when even crooks like to sleep. Our guy was inside somewhere, along with his live-in girlfriend and a couple of kids with uncertain parentage.

Nobody said anything. You could feel the other guys in the "stack" breathing—almost hear them thinking while we waited for the other team to move into position at the back of the place. "Ready?" asked the team leader quietly. Then, "GO! GO! GO!"

"POLICE!" screamed the door-kickers, knocking politely with their thirty-pound ram. The front door exploded inward with a *boom!* from the first impact, bits of the doorjamb flying. The kickers stepped back, and we poured into the residence. I was the number three man in behind the point-man. We penetrated through the living room and down the hall, toward where the bedroom was supposed to be and where our suspect was probably going to be found.

Members of the Reno (Nevada) SWAT team demonstrate a movement technique used in deliberate assaults. Each member has an assigned area of responsibility (AOR). More than any other job in law enforcement, SWAT team members depend on each other for protection and tactical support.

The floor was littered with all kinds of junk: clothing, bottles, plates, each a hazard to navigation. We pushed forward, following the point-man, each covering our danger area. Within maybe two seconds of the door-kick, we were at the bedroom door, and suddenly it flew open. Just as planned, we caught the guy in bed, but now he was halfway up and turning toward us.

The woman was screaming—squealing, really, and you can't really blame her; it was a heck of a way to greet the day. The point-man and the number two guy had both split left and right, respectively, to cover their AORs (areas of responsibility) and then it was just him and me, face to face. He was swearing, I remember, but I can't tell you the words. As he finished turning I saw the gun in his right hand, a *big* revolver, starting to swing up and toward me.

I might have been a fraction of a second ahead of him. My own weapon was a Smith & Wesson Model 3609 9mm auto, at the ready position. I remember that my mind did all the little tricks I was taught it would—the tunnel vision, the slow motion—and I recall watching the Smith come up until the front sight covered his sternum, the white dots of the sight moving into alignment, the texture of the front surface of the trigger as I pushed it. I fired one shot and would have "double-tapped" him if I had the chance, but he went down so fast and hard that it wasn't an option. The woman was screeching now, and the kids were too. Our suspect was sprawled across the bed, onto the floor, as his life drained away.

The SWAT Mission

The incident above was a training exercise, an extremely realistic one intended to train SWAT team members to deal with every awful thing that can, and frequently does, happen to people in the business of crisis intervention and conflict resolution. The bad guy—and the wife, and the kids, too, were all appearing in a very expensive interactive video/computer training system. It provides law enforcement professionals the chance to experience the worst situations and scenarios, to make mistakes, to be killed and then resurrected.

This particular system uses a laser beam inside the pistol and sensors on the screen that pinpoint exactly each impact. On playback we were able to see exactly when I fired and what I hit. One of the lessons I learned was that I don't shoot as well under pressure as I thought. My shot caught the suspect squarely between the eyes; the instructors were impressed, until

Clearing a stairwell. SWAT teams participate in far more close-quarters combat than virtually any contemporary military organization, including outfits like the SEALs and Green Berets, most of whom will never hear a shot fired in anger throughout a whole career. Heckler & Koch, Inc. USA/Steve Galloway

I confessed that I had tried to aim at his sternum, about eighteen inches lower than the point of impact.

The scenario was based on exactly the kind of problems that confront men and women in law enforcement every day, particularly those on the special operations details that are often called SWAT teams. I got to go on that raid, over and over: sometimes the man came up empty-handed—and the wife whipped a gun out from under a pillow, or somebody came out of a closet (with and without a gun); I got a chance to shoot (and avoid shooting) everybody but the kids, and by the time we'd done it a few times I felt like the infant actually had bit me on the leg. It was *that* realistic.

Even though that particular incident was part of a training program, it represents a kind of grim reality for the thousands of men and women police officers in the United States who have to perform these kinds of missions on a regular basis. More and more, these people are officers with extra training, higher standards of performance, and far more challenging duties than officers who never leave patrol. They belong to units with all sorts of different names—some are called SWAT, others used different terms, but they are in just about every jurisdiction around the country. Although the idea is quite new, having been invented only about twenty years ago by the Los Angeles Police Department (LAPD), the time was ripe for it, and the program was quickly adopted almost everywhere.

SWAT teams deal with the nastiest, most dangerous part of law enforcement, the direct confrontation of the most antisocial members of society: snipers, hostage-takers, hijackers, big-time drug dealers, and people who are essentially at war with the rest of society. There are,

The fearsome attire and behavior of SWAT team members has been gradually developed over the past twenty years or so. The vest, the mask, goggles, and especially the big, high capacity Heckler & Koch (H&K) Model USP handgun are all tools of a deadly trade. Heckler & Koch, Inc. USA/Steve Galloway

An H&K MP-5 submachine gun in 10mm caliber. Special weapons in urban and civil law enforcement situations require special tactics. Despite the ability to fire thirty rounds like a "bullet hose," people on

SWAT teams learn to use weapons like this in extremely discriminating and selective ways—and only as a last resort. Heckler & Koch, Inc. USA/Steve Galloway

sadly, an awful lot of people who resort to violence at the drop of a hat. A lot of them have the financial resources to stockpile weapons, legal and illegal. And when provoked, these people quite frequently use those weapons against anyone they consider a threat.

While these problems are not entirely new, the frequency with which law enforcement agencies confront them is far higher than it was in the past. Even small towns have discovered that traditional methods of law enforcement are just inadequate for dealing with these antisocial people and their behavior, and most

have adopted some sort of program for special operations.

Different agencies use their SWAT teams for different kinds of assignments, but the basic set of missions looks like this:

- Counter sniper
- Hostage rescue
- Barricaded suspect
- Probation search
- Search warrant
- Arrest warrant
- Parole search
- Drug raids

And this is what it is all about—the all-too-often cir-cumstance when some person in our society goes vio-lently insane, and is armed, dangerous, and with hostages. Until SWAT teams were invented and de-veloped, there was no coherent way to deal with these people.

These missions can be divided into two basic types, *emergencies* and *deliberate* operations. Deliberate operations—drug raids, "high-risk paper" service—are launched at a time of the team's choosing, and the other is launched to deal with an immediate emergency that someone else—like the Good Guys shootout described in Chapter 3—has precipitated.

SWAT History

The LAPD seems to have been the inventor of the SWAT team, and the name, too, back in 1974. It began, as these things always do, with a series of disasters for law enforcement agencies around the country, and the general realization that traditional, person-to-person law enforcement methods just weren't capable of resolving certain incidents.

One of these incidents developed on a steamy August afternoon in 1966 far from Los Angeles, on the University of Texas campus at Austin. That's when a nice, clean-cut young man named Charles Whitman hauled a box of weapons and ammunition to the top of a 307-foot tower and started indiscriminately shooting people below. Fifteen people were killed and police were held at bay for an hour-and-a-half before Officers Ramiro Martinez and Houston McCoy, and a civilian, Allen Crum, bravely assaulted Whitman's fortified and barricaded position and killed the gunman with two blasts from a shotgun. The incident got the attention of everyone in law enforcement and started many working on innovative ways to deal with similar situations in the future.

Then in January 1972 a clean-cut young black man, a former Navy seaman turned revolutionary named Mark Essex, started a calcu-

lated campaign of assassination directed at whites in general and white policemen specifically. The campaign lasted from New Year's Day until January 7, when it culminated in a battle with New Orleans police. While Essex was finally killed (his body was riddled by bullets over an extended period by over 140 police

Det. Jon Buehler of the Modesto (California) Police Department. Buehler works the white-collar-crime desk, plus the homicide detail; when somebody gets shot in his jurisdiction, he gets to help clean up the mess. Sometimes he helps make it, too. Buehler is one of his department's firearms instructors as well as a sniper on the SWAT team.

Call-outs can be for hasty or deliberate operations. These officers have responded to a call for a barricaded hostage situation in mixed uniforms. Each comes from a different unit within their agency, including robbery, homicide, and gang details; each brings special skills to the team, and each is integrated with the team through a very selective admission process followed by many hours of training.

15

officers when he emerged from his rooftop hiding place), the operation was hardly a model of efficient operations. Among other things, officers fired on each other several times during the operation, and during a final—and unnecessary since Essex was long since dead—assault, nine officers were wounded by police gunfire. Over 600 police officers, plus helicopters and Federal Bureau of Investigation (FBI) and Treasury agents, participated in the operation against a lone gunman who had killed a dozen people and left twelve wounded seriously. It was not an operation that anybody wanted to go through again.

These incidents, plus the Watts riots and similar disorders, were the beginning, but there were other incidents that former LAPD Chief of Police Daryl Gates cites in his autobiography, *Chief*, as instrumental in the development of the SWAT team concept. The LAPD had started working on a special operations capability as early as 1967, adapting military tactics and technologies to certain new kinds of urban, civil warfare that just didn't fit the training and pro-

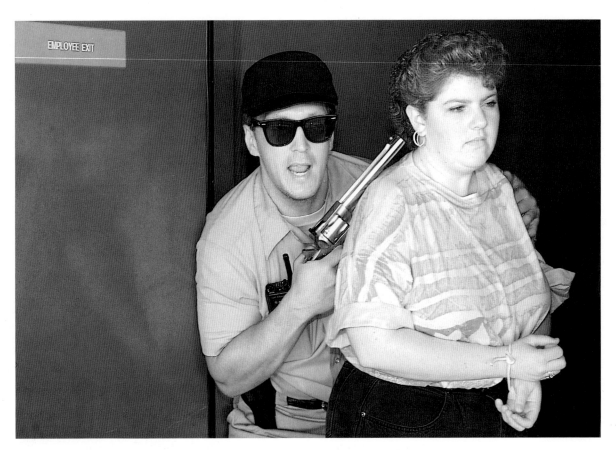

Although the suspect (an officer role-playing in an exercise) might think he's safe behind his victim, any moderately competent SWAT sniper within 200 meters should be able to drop him with the first shot, and drop him so cleanly that his trigger finger won't even twitch. This kind of capability is the result of training, selection, and equipment—plus enlightened command and control.

16

Moving up. When the team is called out on a situation like a hostage-taking, the patrol division (the normal uniformed cops cruising the streets, taking calls for service) will have already secured the perimeter. SWAT comes in later, taking over the operation only when all the approvals have been made and the departmental standard operating procedures (SOP) list is fulfilled.

One of the special SWAT weapons is a modified version of the military M-16 rifle, the CAR-15. This one is coming up from the "ready" position to engage a *suspect in a training exercise. The little flashlight on the fore-end is operated with a pressure-sensitive finger switch on the upper hand guard.*

cedures of the past.

In 1967 there was an incident in which a barricaded suspect managed to hold off large numbers of the LAPD patrol division for a while, wounding three of the patrol officers plus a civilian before the suspect was captured. Gates realized his department just wasn't prepared to deal with snipers or barricaded suspects, so Gates and the LAPD started to find a solution.

With the help of some officers with prior military service and the cooperation of some nearby Marines, an LAPD unit began to train to deal with snipers and suspects in fortified buildings. Over a period of time they developed a doctrine that adapted some military tactics

and weapons to civil situations. It was just in time.

By 1967 the department had trained and equipped sixty officers and collected them into their own dedicated unit, a third Metro division platoon called D-Platoon. The unit was organized into six squads, each with five members—a leader, a sniper, an observer, a scout, and a rear-guard.

Gates wanted to call the unit SWAT from the beginning, and that was fine with then-Chief Ed Davis—until he found out what it stood for. When told the letters represented *Special Weapons Attack Teams* he immediately rejected the name as entirely too military. But Davis accepted the acronym after Gates and his

Participation on a SWAT team isn't for all officers in a police department. In fact, it is normally a volunteer assignment that adds plenty of extra burdens on a career, sometimes without any additional pay. In the best teams, membership is much more than just voluntary—it is an elite unit with extremely high standards for admission and retention, a set of "zero defects" people who work hard to get on the team and work harder to stay on it.

colleagues modified it to *Special Weapons And Tactics.*

Although accepted in concept by LAPD's Chief, the new SWAT team wasn't accepted by many of the leaders or the rank and file of the department of the day, and according to Gates' account of those years, the unit practiced in secret well away from the rest of the department.

Originally the unit was intended to deal

The basic unit of a SWAT team isn't the individual but the "buddy team," or two-officer pair. These two are moving in on a barricaded suspect along with about twenty other officers.

19

Planning and coordination are part of the SWAT operator's art, the foundation for executing missions with safety and dispatch. Here the team sergeant is briefing the team on the layout of a building before they launch the mission.

with barricaded snipers, but it didn't take long for the LAPD to figure out that hostage rescue would naturally be part of the tactical plan in many real-world scenarios, and they started planning and training accordingly, often using Gates as the hostage. Their equipment was bought at surplus stores, paid for out of the officers' own pockets. Other equipment and weapons were improvised and assembled by members of the unit: scaling ladders, sniper rifles, uniforms, surveillance systems, and all the other miscellaneous gear that has since become standard.

The standard operating procedures (SOP) that the LAPD developed have proven to be sound and remain the model for many teams and departments in the United States today. When an incident develops that fits the criteria for a SWAT call-out, the field commander makes the initial request for SWAT assistance. Within a half-hour, two of the five-man teams are normally on-scene. They develop a plan and present it to the field commander; if the commander approves, SWAT takes over the operation from the patrol division.

The LAPD used their newly invented SWAT team for the first time on December 8, 1969, against a heavily fortified building at

In the first minutes and hours of a SWAT operation, while bystanders are fretting about what they think is police inactivity and inattention, the team is busy plotting and scheming somewhere, spending hours *perhaps, preparing for the sixty seconds or so that will carry them from the beginning of their assault to its final conclusion.*

4115 South Central Avenue, occupied by a large number of well-armed Black Panthers. The SWAT team staged the operation at 0500 hours at an armory in Chavez ravine; using the patrol division to set up a perimeter and isolate the address, the forty-member team prepared to execute two arrest warrants on Panthers who had threatened to kill a police officer a week previously.

When the team attempted to serve the warrants, the Panthers opened fire with two dozen weapons, including thirteen rifles, five shotguns, five handguns, plus a .45cal Thompson submachine gun. Three officers were hit, one

taking six rounds. The wounded officers were extracted and the SWAT team pulled back to positions around the building.

The police and Panthers exchanged fire for hours. The building had been fortified to prevent a simple assault from breaking in, and a stand-off developed. The SWAT team discovered that they had planned for a lot of contingencies, but not this one. Phone calls were made to acquire authorization to get and use an M79 grenade launcher, a military shoulder weapon that—if available—would have punched a hole through the building's steel plate and masonry, which was impenetrable by

They say you've got to knock on the door first, but they don't tell you how loud. That fireball is from a coil of detonating ("det") cord, prepared for cutting a hole in a wooden door; it is just one novel way SWAT teams use to gain entry to a structure. The essence of an assault is speed and shock—both of which help save lives instead of lose them.

small arms fire. However, before the M79 could be authorized and delivered, after a siege lasting all morning, the Panthers elected to surrender. Six people were arrested, three of them were wounded. The first SWAT mission was a victory, in spite of everything.

SLA Shoot-out

While the Black Panther operation was successful, it was only a dry-run compared to the operation that brought the SWAT concept to national and international attention five years later. In May 1974, the LAPD and its now experienced and professional SWAT team confronted the Simbionese Liberation Army, a tiny group of violent radicals that had been confounding the entire American law enforcement community when it abducted Patty Hearst.

The Modesto SWAT team. Participation is voluntary, the standards are high, the extra pay is nonexistent.

In case you've forgotten, the SLA was a group that, among other things, gunned down the school superintendent of Oakland with a cyanide-tipped bullet, robbed banks, shot store clerks, and kidnapped the Hearst heiress — who was kept in a closet for weeks, raped, and then converted to participate in robberies—all in the name of righting some imaginary injustices. It was the kind of behavior calculated to attract a lot of attention from law enforcement agencies, and that attention finally paid off.

The FBI discovered that the prime figures of the SLA, William and Emily Harris, were in the Los Angeles area in early May 1974 when the couple were identified as the people who got into a scuffle with a sporting goods store clerk. The feds turned up the heat and quickly started generating productive leads. They raided the house where the Harrises had been staying—and just missed them, and then identified four other addresses as possible hiding places. The FBI and LAPD SWAT started planning to take them down.

While the planning proceeded, the SWAT team got a surveillance report from one of the addresses: *This is the place, the SLA are inside now*.

The operation kicked off at 1730 hours. Over two hundred patrol officers set up the perimeter around 1466 East 54th Street, an inconspicuous little Los Angeles bungalow in a quiet residential neighborhood. With a command post (CP) two blocks away, the SWAT team elements, a total of twenty-five officers, started slipping into their positions five minutes later at 1735.

Team One deployed to the front and one side of the house, Team Two to the rear and other side. Each team consisted of four two-officer pairs. Each team carried M16s, tear gas projectors, one sniper rifle, plus each officer's pistol for backup. At about 1740 hours the leader of Team One, Sgt. Ron McCarthy, used a bullhorn to demand that the residents of the structure surrender. All he got for his efforts was one somewhat bewildered eight-year-old boy.

The tear gas went in shortly after that. The response was a long blast of automatic weapons

An officer pair provide absolute physical control and security for this hallway and for each other against all comers. Those shotguns will reliably cut down anyone within ten or fifteen meters.

fire from a Browning Automatic Rifle. The BAR is a legendary weapon, a big rifle that fires .30-06 rounds from a 20-round box magazine like a machine gun. It was a favorite infantry weapon during World War II; it was a horrifying weapon for the SWAT team members receiving its fire.

The SLA people inside the house and the SWAT team outside exchanged fire for about fifty minutes before flames appeared at the front of the building. It was fully involved within a minute. The people inside kept firing for another few minutes, then the firing stopped. It took ten minutes for the house to burn to the ground, and nobody came out. That was the end of the Simbionese Liberation Army and the beginning of the SWAT legend. When the crooks and the cops finally confronted each other, LAPD's SWAT team showed the cops were going to win. It was an object lesson to crooks and crazies everywhere.

Into the Mainstream

SWAT teams have been common for only about twenty years, but in that short time they have become an essential part of most urban law enforcement organizations. They are known by many names, but the basic idea behind each is the same: a small, specially trained, equipped, and deployed group of officers used for the riskiest missions and the most

It is hard to believe that all these people can make an assault in absolute silence, but they do; communications are done with whispers and hand signals, radio reception is through ear pieces. Personal equipment is

all set up to eliminate squeaks and rattles, and boots all have soft, smooth soles. The result is what one department calls a "stealth to contact" movement technique.

challenging situations. They may be called MERGE, CERT, SWAT, or all sorts of other acronyms, but they are the specialists within police and sheriff's departments who are called out to deal with barricaded suspects, high-risk arrest warrant service, hostage takers, snipers, drug labs, and the protection of distinguished visitors.

Despite all the media attention, the television series, and the regular appearance of these teams in the news, very few US police departments still have a full fledged SWAT team. In fact, ninety percent of all departments in the United States have less than twenty full-time officers, and most of those have less than ten people. But even these small departments often have some sort of contingency for dealing with situations that require special weapons and tactics; generally, they call in neighboring agency personnel or teams.

The very idea of these special operations teams has been, and still is, controversial. Police work is driven in every community at least partly by politics. And many politicians don't like the idea of these apparently para-military groups, with their ninja-style uniforms, automatic weapons, and seemingly violent approach to conflict resolution. There were howls of protest when the first team was assembled and deployed in Los Angeles, and there have been howls from just about every other jurisdiction that has adopted them. And, there are continuing efforts to subvert them, one way or another, by some police chiefs and politicians who seem to want to wish the need for them away.

These teams are organized and employed differently by every jurisdiction that uses them. In some cases, particularly in the bigger departments, they are staffed by officers whose full-time assignment is to the teams. In other cases, SWAT team members are patrol officers, detectives, or assigned to homicide, administration, or other units within the department, and perform on the team as a collateral duty.

SWAT Missions Within Police Agencies

To appreciate and understand how SWAT teams function, you first need an understanding of the mission of the larger police agency that sponsors the team and provides its resources, people, direction, and management. Although that department might have 200 members or 10,000, the principles will be the same, and the basic missions will be, too. Here, then, is a short course in law enforcement and the role of SWAT teams within it.

Within each department there are several basic missions; *patrol* is the largest in virtually every case. In addition, departments normally

The inner perimeter is secured against entry or exit, sometimes by members of the police department's patrol division, sometimes by members of the special operations team. It can be stunningly boring work, until somebody tries to break out—and then the job becomes quite interesting.

25

RON MARTINELLI, PH.D.—
CRIMINOLOGIST, POLICE TRAINER, AND STREET COP

"I believe people develop a criminal attitude as children," Martinelli says, "as a reaction to their environment. That environment is their immediate family and their friends and associates. I've found that there are people who will commit crimes of passion—you come home one day and find a guy in bed with your wife, and you blow them both away, or your kids are starving and you rob a liquor store to get money to feed them—those are tremendous lapses of judgment and are serious crimes, but you can understand their motivation. The chance that such a person would commit a similar crime in the future is relatively small. Only about 15 percent of people in jail fall into this category. The other 85 percent are the hard-core criminal element who view criminal activity as a profession. They thrive on the totality of criminality and violence. They revel in the victimization they inflict—serial rapists, serial killers, bank robbers, burglars —they thrive on their accomplishments. They cause us the greatest concern, and they commit—by far—the greatest amount of crime that we have to deal with.

"When you incarcerate these people, when you put them in jail, they almost never change. Exhaustive studies have shown that about 88 percent of these people return to serious crime within a year of release, most within six months.

"When they are rearrested and convicted, they treat prison as a kind of university and study what they did wrong to get arrested. I've dealt with a lot of people who are candid about this. Their resolve isn't to observe the laws after they're released, but to not get caught again. In prison, burglars sit with burglars, robbers with robbers, murderers stay together, just as the 'white collar' criminals and dope dealers, and they all are trying to learn ways to commit these crimes better in the future. Very few are remorseful.

"These people have made cognizant choices—to stay in school or leave, to take drugs or abstain, to commit crimes or not, to be with good people or bad. In a lot of cases, of course, these people come from homes where the parents belong in jail for their neglect of these people as children. But you can always find people who have grown up in the worst of circumstances, who have never committed a crime and who have led successful lives.

"The police officer today needs to be a kind of jack-of-all-trades: good at dealing with people, a good investigator, a good tactician, knowledgeable about a wide variety of weapons, of criminal behavior, and the law. Unfortunately, not too many officers are like that. We tend to pigeonhole ourselves into specialties. It is a big mistake when we sell ourselves short in this business.

"So not everybody is attracted to special operations. It takes a particular kind of officer to be in special operations, one with plenty of experience and skills, plus a desire to be part of a unit with extremely high standards. Not everybody is suited for special ops. It takes a person who is a good team player, someone who is very patient, highly skilled in basic police procedures and then in specialist techniques. You have to be motivated, enthusiastic, highly trained, and cross-trained in a variety of skills. You have to be able to work as a reliable component of a team—under the most stressful of circumstances, while bullets are being fired and people are screaming. You have to be able to function while extremely uncomfortable—to lie in one spot for hours, under the hot sun, and not move. You have to stay still, wait for hours, for that one moment when you have to do your job perfectly well, the first time—the only time. That is what a basic SWAT officer has to be.

"Police officers tend to be 'co-dependent.' We rely on each other as a matter of routine. But a SWAT officer has to be able to function as a highly independent person, sometimes for extended periods, without any supervision and while still being a member of the team."

An old city bus has been rebuilt and adapted to serve as a command post, complete with mobile telephone and radio communications, a desk for the hostage negotiation team, a coffee maker and—most important during those long, long stand-offs—a toilet. Instead of trying to adapt an old bus, most cities use huge mobile homes for their command posts.

have homicide, detective, sex crimes, and other units, each specializing in particular enforcement problems. Until about twenty years ago these traditional units were perfectly adequate to deal with the criminal activity of American cities.

One experienced officer explains: "The basic mission of law enforcement is pretty much just what it says on the door: To Protect and Serve. The philosophies and techniques change over the years—like 'community-based law enforcement' today—but the basic premise of our work as police is to protect the public, to ensure their physical safety. Originally, we were reactive, we waited until there was a problem and then we reacted by going off and trying to deal with it. We didn't think we needed to work with the community; that's changed tremendously.

"Our culture has changed tremendously over the last couple of decades. The nature and amount of criminal activity has intensified greatly. The criminal justice system hasn't coped effectively, with the result that the cop on the street has a bigger problem than ever. But that has forced us to be creative, to look at the problems carefully and to develop new ways of dealing with them. Instead of waiting for a house to be burglarized, we now study the behavior of drug users, the appearance of people under the influence of drugs, and we try to intercept the problem before it turns into a burglary."

Det. Jon Buehler carries most of his gear with him all the time, safely stowed in the truck of his car.

A three-officer element uses a corner for cover and concealment. The number two man provides rear security for the point man

When a suspect is barricaded in a large building (in this case, a hotel) rooms are cleared individually, methodically, and in silence. The point man's hand-and-arm signal silently indicates "unknown" situation ahead.

Rick Martinelli demonstrates the proper carry for the MP-5—trigger finger out of the guard, alongside the receiver, muzzle slightly lowered for improved visibility, both eyes wide open, and left hand and arm supporting the weapon from below. Martinelli can maintain this alert posture for many minutes; it is reasonably safe but still allows him to engage in under a second. When he must fire, Martinelli can selectively fire one, two or more rounds from the submachine gun, and all will probably hit where he aims. His department standard is zero misses. Since the weapon is suppressed, the loudest noise from the engagement will come from the impact of the bullets on the target, and the suspect's body hitting the ground.

Instead of the kind of casual patrol that was once the police officer's job, law enforcement jurisdictions around the United States are actively seeking out the people and organizations that commit crimes as part of their routine. As one officer says, "Instead of waiting for a car bomb to go off, we infiltrate the gangs to find out about these things before they happen. That's what 'pro-active' policing is all about."

SWAT teams are both pro-active and reactive. The special operations units within police departments constantly prepare for events that might happen—the crazed gunman who decides to arbitrarily kill people, or the methodical assassin who stalks political figures.

Chapter 2

Missions and Organization

Different cities use their special operations teams in different ways. Some, like San Jose and Los Angeles, have a dedicated unit (called SWAT at LAPD, and MERGE, or Mobile Emergency Response Group & Equipment, in San Jose). Even though the members of San Jose's MERGE unit are full-time special operators, they—like virtually all SWAT team members elsewhere—have a set of collateral duties. How the team is set up and deployed will vary with local conditions. Both San Jose and Los Angeles have major Mexican and Asian gang problems.

In the San Jose Police Department MERGE unit, whose volunteer members serve for three years and then go off to other assignments, call-outs occur about once a month. San Jose maintains two ten-officer teams, with five "partner" teams within each unit. These two-officer units are always busy doing tactical patrol, working on investigations, studying individuals, looking for trouble before the trouble starts. They work what is called the "tactical patrol" end of special investigations. In San Jose's case, they are tasked with investigations or initiate investigations on their own.

Target shooters get to stand in one spot and bang away, but SWAT shooters learn to run and shoot. The drill begins with the officers running short distances. The runs progress to fifty meters. The officers engage the target at the end of each run, and no misses are tolerated.

The LAPD draws from the Metro Division, the same kind of patrol division that, in uniform or in plainclothes, spends its time out on the streets looking for trouble. Reno, Nevada, has a small department whose SWAT team has an excellent reputation. They are called out several times a month. Other jurisdictions, like the LAPD, can get called out almost once a day.

Basics

SWAT teams are typically organized in a "building block" pattern. There will be a commander or team leader, plus a number of entry/arrest teams, perimeter teams, and sniper/observer teams. These entry and sniper elements are built up from small "buddy teams" of two officers who will normally deploy together, as a unit. As an example, one rural California county sheriff's department operates a twelve-officer team with three sniper/observer teams (six officers) and three entry/arrest teams (another six), plus the commander.

Training

Most teams will send its members to one of the schools conducted by the FBI, by the larger jurisdictions, and by private criminal justice trainers that offer classes in the basics and in the specialties of special operations. The basic course is normally one to two weeks long. Advanced courses are attended by experienced team members; these include classes in the use of chemical agents, surveillance techniques, demolitions, booby traps, and all sorts of other specialties. SWAT team leaders attend classes that train them in techniques for special situations they may confront, and include courses in critical incident command, special operations planning, and the execution of high-risk raids.

Snipers learn their art in additional class-

Sgt. Diane Jones earned a spot on her department's team by meeting the same physical standards as the men. Normally departments have lower physical standards for women, but Sergeant Jones can do more chin-ups than you or I can, and came close to making the Olympic discus team a few years ago. By performing at the same high level as anyone else, Sergeant Jones has earned the respect and acceptance of most of the men in her department.

es. The FBI conducts a basic sniper/observer course for law enforcement personnel, as do several private organizations, including the National Rifle Association (NRA). The US Marine Corps also offers advanced sniper training for SWAT teams and other law enforcement personnel. Many snipers continue to hone their skills by training with the Army, or the Green Berets or other military special operators at Fort Bragg, North Carolina, and the Special Operations Target Interdiction Course.

Applying for the Team

Police departments treat membership on SWAT teams differently; in some departments, it is an assignment, part of the normal career progression that everybody is expected to go through. In these departments, participation may be limited to two or three years, after which you move on to burglary, homicide, or other units. Everybody is expected to gain familiarity with the special operations unit— whether they want it or not. And in some cases they don't. But generally, assignment to the team is an honor reserved for the cream of the department, the men and women who are the most aggressive, intelligent, and professional. That's partly because only people with a high level of motivation and energy can put up with the pressures and the extra responsibilities— and partly because the costs of a bad op can be so high that it is necessary to have only the most reliable and skilled people.

As a result, most departments make membership on the team difficult to attain and difficult to maintain. As one sniper explains, "You don't get selected for the team unless you have already demonstrated *exceptional* marksmanship skills."

Other standards for admission are extremely high, physically, emotionally, and in almost every other way. Most departments select people with proven reliability, officers without drinking problems or family problems—someone who is very stable, patient, in good physical condition, and highly skilled in basic police procedures.

Some departments set extremely high stan-

Membership on the Reno team is considered a privilege that must be earned rather than a duty to be endured. Each member is tested monthly in an intensive program that includes physical fitness, combat shooting, and department rules and regulations.

dards for physical fitness and tactical proficiency, with membership on the team treated like a very special privilege reserved only for the most motivated. The Reno team is one of these; the team trains together regularly, starting with a half-hour of military-style physical training (PT) and then a two-mile run across the desert. Then there are classes and live-fire tactical training. Team members are frequently tested and evaluated; the minimum passing score is 100 percent.

Much of the training is done in-house, with the more experienced and more highly trained people conducting classes for newcomers. And, as far as that goes, there is considerable cross-training done on the teams, with the entry/ar-

rest officers studying the skills and techniques of the sniper/observers, too.

You would think that with such high standards, extra responsibilities, and a higher level of inherent danger that membership on a team would rate a financial bonus, and it usually does. But the amount can vary tremendously; one sheriff's department pays its SWAT team members an extra $33 per month. "That doesn't even cover a tiny fraction of the money I spend on my equipment," one officer says. Such an amount is near the low end of the spectrum, however, and reflects the difficulty some department have with funding rather than hostility toward their team. Other departments are much more generous. On the other hand,

33

Part of the Reno SWAT team.

Modesto doesn't pay its officers a dime to be on the team.

Call-out Considerations

When an incident starts to perk, most people on the team will know about it pretty quickly. It will be on the radio, and anyone on patrol will hear about it that way. For other members of the team who may have the day off, or who are working desk jobs or other assignments, their pagers will go off, sometimes well in advance of any decision to actually call out the team. This early notification is merely an alert to put the team on notice that they had better cancel the wedding anniversary dinner reservations at that fancy restaurant downtown and stick close to the phone.

As the incident heats up or cools off, the watch commander will be deciding whether the team gets called out or not. It isn't always a clear-cut decision. One officer remarks:

"I don't think you need to call out a SWAT team every time you have a burglar barricaded inside a store or a residence. But on the other hand, there is some civil liability if you don't call out the team and then someone gets killed.

"Most situations can be resolved by normal police officers. Because of budget constraints, our department is reluctant to call out the team; their tendency is to try to resolve it with more patrol officers—and frequently they do. It has gotten to the point where it takes an exceptional situation to call out our team. For instance, we had a man who murdered three people here in one community, went up the road to another community and killed two more, then took a hostage at a house—and our [county sheriff's] department was never called out. They just surrounded the place with patrol officers and when somebody called in to talk to him, the guy realized he was surrounded and shot himself in the head. So we have gone to the extreme of hardly ever calling the team out.

"Most agencies—if they even have a SWAT team—make the team assignment a collateral duty. We just can't afford to take people off patrol and make them work SWAT fulltime, although that is really the way it ought to be

34

done because of the intense training and preparation that needs to be done. These guys need to be training all the time, and if you are working patrol or detective, you just don't have that opportunity. For an entry guy, being able to shoot 'center-of-mass' may not be good enough when you are confronted with a hostage situation."

For individual officers, call-out really begins *inside*, with a frame of mind. One officer says that he starts every shift by looking at pictures in his locker. Instead of the girlie shots some officers tape up, this officer put up pictures of violent crooks he knew were in and around his beat, the guys he wanted to find. He also had pictures of his family posted on his locker door, too, reminding him of his obligations at home. "I went through a regular ritual, every day, of looking at those pictures while I put on my vest," he says.

Call-Up

The decision process involved in designating an incident a SWAT mission is administratively and politically complex. There are all sorts of turfs and territories. If a watch commander asks for a SWAT evaluation of an event, he may be considered a weak leader who lacks confidence in himself and his patrol division. Then there is the cost, which can run up thousands of extra dollars for overtime and other costs, whether or not the SWAT team actually is used to resolve the incident. So the tactical problem of putting the team in the picture is extremely sticky.

Some team members find themselves being asked to play their SWAT team role without having the rest of the team on the operation, a situation that just drives a team commander nuts. That's because there is a lot of confusion during a tense operation, and sometimes watch commanders and patrol division sergeants will mistakenly think the team is a player on an op when it actually hasn't been called out. During one incident, three team members participated as players within their normal patrol function, but in the post-operation review the incident commander stated that he had three SWAT

Reno SWAT begins its training days with a little jog around the desert. The temperature is in the upper eighties on an early August morning. They will run a three-mile course—as a team—across the flats and up into the hills behind their range. Most members sensibly remove their shirts—all except Sgt. Linda Shepherd.

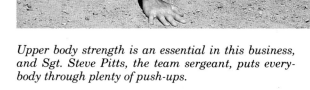

The team does about an hour of physical training (PT), starting with plenty of stretching exercises.

Upper body strength is an essential in this business, and Sgt. Steve Pitts, the team sergeant, puts everybody through plenty of push-ups.

teams participating.

After that incident, the team commander had a chat with the chief of police, which resulted in a directive and this little speech to the team: "This is an order—a *direct* order! There is no flexibility, no latitude on this: the presence of a SWAT team member, or several SWAT team members *does not* constitute the presence of the SWAT team! Unless I, as team commander, or one of the five team sergeants has agreed and is en route, there is no team participation, no deployment without our approval and authorization."

The point the team commander is making is that there is a significant difference between the skills of the officers when used as part of the patrol division and when used within the specialized command and control of a SWAT team. Unfortunately, the pressure of events often encourages sergeants and lieutenants to use the members of the team in adhoc special operations—much to the annoyance of the team leaders. These pressures may be financial or political.

As a result, in some departments all team members are instructed to be alert to situations that might result in a call-out, and to notify the team leadership early, just in case. "If you are sitting on an outside perimeter and see something going down that ought to indicate a call-out, 'drop a dime' to one of us and let us know," one team sergeant says. "I wear my pager in the shower," another team leader says, "I am *not* difficult to get ahold of."

Another team member discusses the different philosophies of people on patrol and people with special operations duties:

"There are a lot of good coppers out there, but they just don't have the organization, training, and equipment that we have. Or the accountability, either. We on the team evaluate situations based on worst-case scenarios, but the patrol division commanders tend to do the opposite. They tend to think of the easiest ways to get out of a situation, to underestimate the situation, and to miss danger signals. In our department we're encouraged to go up to them and say, "Maybe you aren't seeing this situa-

Combat pistol technique is another essential for team members. The team members each work through several long drills and a variety of situations and sce- *narios, all based on doctrine from Gunsite, the revered institution of higher combat shooting.*

tion over here—this might be something you should consider for a SWAT call-out."

Then there are the departments that don't want to call out their teams for anything. A member of one of these reports, "If our department has a high-risk search warrant, the tendency is to do it with patrol officers, rather than with the team. There seems to be a bit of jealousy operating. Some of the watch commanders, the captains and lieutenants, appear to have an aversion of what they seem to think are hot shots and elitists on the SWAT team,

that they can get along just fine without them,and avoid calling us out."

On the other hand, for a team to have credibility within a department, it can't cry wolf too often. When the team leader makes the assessment that the team needs to be called out, the post-event review had better justify the call-out.

Call-Out

The SWAT team isn't called out by the dispatchers (who may pass on a command), but by the on-scene commander, who actually makes

One of the combat drills the Reno team uses prepares members of assault teams for selecting and engaging targets with speed and precision. The drill involves an actual assault on a room with targets on the walls representing hostage-taking crooks; near the targets, though, are people role-playing hostages. The shooters carry submachine guns and handguns; they must engage the small, 6in-diameter targets without shooting their friends—and the standard for the exercise is no misses; all shots must be on target.

the decision. It is a critical decision and sets in motion a complex, and sometimes expensive, set of procedures. During the hour or more it will take the team to arrive, the patrol officers maintain and develop their perimeter, securing the scene; they isolate the problem as much as possible, and sort out and rescue any victims if possible; and they continue to collect information about the source and location of the problem.

The members of the SWAT team will receive notification in various ways, some over the radio, others with a phone call or a pager alert. The two-officer teams working out of cars will already know something about the incident because they will have heard the radio traffic, but others, who may be working at desk jobs will know nothing of the incident until they arrive downtown or at the incident command center.

Different cities handle the call-out in different ways. Some officers carry their gear and weapons with them in the trunks of their cars; others keep everything in a locker at the department headquarters. These lockers are typically deep within the building, behind layers of heavy doors with crypto locks. That's because there is usually a large collection of heavy firepower stored along with the uniforms and radios. Nearly all SWAT teams maintain inventories of exotic weapons: Uzi submachine pistols, the superb German MP5 9mm submachine gun (with or without a sound suppresser that makes the weapon nearly silent), riot shotguns, and CAR-15 rifles (the compact version of the military M-16 rifle).

Team members change from their patrol uniform or plain clothes into their SWAT uniform in the locker room or at the incident command center at the scene. The standard SWAT uniform is a dark coverall or two-piece outfit, sometimes a military flight suit. Lightweight body armor is worn under the coverall, protecting the chest. Boots are worn, but instead of the heavy, leather variety used by the military, a lighter type (HiTec or Rocky brands) are preferred. Pistol belts with weapon and accessory magazines are buckled on next. Finally, the assault vest with radio, extra ammunition for pistol and shoulder weapon, handcuffs, and specialized equipment are added.

The team is assembled and transported to the CP where they will take over the responsibility for the tactical phase of the operation from the patrol division. The CP will be the focus of the operation until its completion. The operation will stage in and out of the CP, which is usually a cluster of specially converted vehicles designed for such a response.

Setting up the CP is one of the first important elements of a SWAT mission. The CP needs to be very close to the incident location and yet remain secure from the suspects' gunfire. Typically the CP is a block or so from the location, with room for parking the numerous vehicles that will be arriving. It helps to have electrical power, but generators aboard the vans are normally not available to serve that function.

All officers and emergency equipment will use the CP as a known location for staging. The hostage negotiator and incident commander will work out of the CP. Solving numerous logistical problems associated with a special op is part of the CP function. Since these ops last for many hours, provisions for feeding people must be part of the plan, along with arrangements for toilet facilities. A press officer will use the CP to provide information to the news media.

Early in the operation, the SWAT team commander will usually issue a hasty plan for emergencies. If the suspect starts shooting hostages, for example, the entry teams may have to make an assault without full preparation and planning.

The sniper/observer teams will be deployed and eventually report back to the CP with a mass of detail. Fairly quickly, a detailed diagram of the location will be drawn. A large support staff helps the SWAT team by establishing voice contact with the suspect (if possible), running information through databases, and stitching together a mass of information.

Every attempt is made to resolve the incident without an assault, but while everybody hopes for the best, they plan for the worst. The hostage negotiator will try to convince the suspect to surrender. While that is happening the entry team will be plotting and scheming about how to assault the building. Gradually, a plan will develop for the assault. The plan will be rehearsed on or near the site, refined, and rehearsed again, over and over, until it becomes nearly automatic.

Officer Preparation

"My partner and I do something I think all officer teams ought to do all the time "said one officer." We call it the *what if* game. While we're driving around, we work out contingency plans for *everything*. What if you get in a gunfight while you're driving? We found a place to practice our tactical driving skills, and we develop our own SOPs for what we will do when that happens. What if you get shot in the arm? The leg? So we practice shooting from 'wounded' positions. We set our vehicle up as if our lives depended on it; what if you are blinded, can you get into the trunk of the car? Can you find what you need? That's what officers need to do; if you are going to take this job you ought to do it with complete dedication.

Another combat drill: buddy teams run and shoot past each other in alternating leapfrog moves forward, and then in retreat. It is physically demanding, difficult shooting; again, Sergeant Pitts keeps yelling, "No misses!"

"When you have a good team and it clicks, there is nothing better. A team has to be cohesive, flexible, fluid, and have complete mutual trust. If somebody isn't up to standard they shouldn't be on the team. Nobody should be on a team for political reasons. Our department did that a few years ago when some people, who didn't want to be on the SWAT team, were brought on because of their race and gender—they were disliked by the team, they didn't do their jobs, and they weren't happy. Since then we've had other people, particularly one female officer, who've been highly successful on the team because she *wanted* to be part of the unit, and they worked hard to meet the standard. They earned their spot and were respected as a result."

The SOP

Police special operations are governed by SOPs. A typical call-out might involve a situation where a man with a gun enters a building, shoots people, and then confronts authorities. Variations on the theme are all too common,

While the rest of the team is running around in the Nevada heat, Det. Chris Carter prepares a coil of det cord for busting open a door. Carter is a former member of the most respected of all SWAT teams any- *where, the British Army's Special Air Service (SAS). Now he's a detective in the robbery/homicide division of his department, and an explosives specialist for the team.*

41

and when they happen, the following describes how police departments typically deal with them.

The Comm Center

A dispatcher in an emergency communications office receives a call on a 911 line. The caller may be completely hysterical or as cool as ice. In most major metropolitan areas the dispatcher's computer screen will display the phone number and street address of the caller, and the system will have the capability of locking the line open, even if the receiver is put down.

Once the dispatcher understands the nature of the complaint, she pushes a red button

to immediately summon a supervisor. The dispatcher or supervisor will maintain contact with the caller while pulling out a book with a list of SOPs for this type of call. The book contains SOPs for all sorts of emergencies, from women in advanced labor, to plane crashes; the dispatcher turns to the page for barricaded hostage situations and starts working down the list from top to bottom.

Some SOPs involve requests for information from the caller, while others indicate actions to be taken by the dispatcher. One of the first actions will be a radio transmission that every officer on the street will hear: "Man with a gun, shots fired, 111 California Street, seventeenth floor. This operation will be handled on TAC One [tactical channel one]; all other traffic switch to TAC Two."

The channel is now cleared and dedicated to this one emergency, with no distractions. The dispatcher and supervisor team will work the call until it is over.

The first objective of the game is to determine the nature of the problem—exactly what is happening, where the problem is, who is causing the problem, and who the victims are. The dispatcher will need to collect extremely important information, under the most difficult of circumstances. What kind of building is the incident in? (A high-rise office building is the worst.) Has anybody been shot? How many gunmen are there? What do they look like? Do you know them by name? What do the guns look like? Where are the gunmen now? Are there hostages? Are the gunmen moving around, or are they staying in one place?

While the dispatcher gathers information, the dispatch supervisor begins working on a preliminary contingency plan. Does the SWAT team need to be notified? Will a helicopter be needed? Where should the CP be located?

Even before the SWAT team is notified, the supervisor starts working the chain of command, notifying the watch commander and other officials on the SOP. The dispatcher and supervisor start calculating staffing requirements

An entry team practices assaults with explosives. While the blast is rather dramatic, and noisy too, it is safer than anything else for some situations, for the people who make the assault as well as for those inside. The blast will provide enough noise and chaos to keep the residents confused for ten seconds or more, long enough to let the team get them proned out and cuffed before anybody needs to get shot.

An observer delivers a report to the command post (CP). Sgt. Mike Zahr's (left) vest carries spare magazines for his Uzi. The magazines serve two purposes: *the first is to feed the gun, the second is to provide a little extra armor for the sergeant's vitals. The sergeant also wears a throat mike for his radio.*

for the call, with plans for backup from adjacent jurisdictions if the operation will use up the available officers on the street.

When the situation becomes known, the communications supervisor will initiate the request that the SWAT team be *notified*. The decision to actually use the team will not be the dispatcher's, but usually the watch commander's. This early notification is essential because, even under the best of circumstances, a team cannot be expected to arrive on scene in less than an hour.

Often it takes much longer than an hour for a team to assemble since its members will be spread out all over the city, involved in a

dozen different activities. They all must stop what they're doing and sometimes will have to come back into headquarters, change into their tactical uniforms, collect weapons, and attend a briefing. To speed things up, many departments require team members to keep their gear in their cars at all times so they can respond to incidents directly, without bothering to collect weapons and uniforms downtown.

A major incident like this one will prompt the dispatch supervisor to call for fire apparatus and paramedics. Their ladders, lights, and ambulances can be essential items of equipment. Also, fires are often started as a result of these incidents (by tear gas grenades and flash-bang grenades in particular), and fire engines nearby can reduce the loss of life.

While the SWAT team is being called in, the incident commander at first will probably be the sergeant who is responsible for the patrol area where the incident occurred. The sergeant will soon be relieved by the lieutenant who serves as watch commander during this shift. In some jurisdictions, the incident commander will be specified as a captain, probably the commander of the field operations division. But this isn't always such a hot idea; as one officer observes, "The higher up the chain of command you go the less recent training and tactical experience you are likely to have. Captains just don't have a lot of recent street experience! The highest rank an incident commander should have, I think, is *lieutenant*, somebody who is in the field, with plenty of experience and knowledge of the SOPs."

Radio Traffic

During the early phase of an event that will require call-out of a special operations team, the performance of the dispatcher and first officers on the scene is particularly critical. They set the tone of the operation with their attitude and the way they work through the SOP. Often, even experienced officers and emergency dispatchers will sound excited, even panicked on the radio.

"The dispatchers control the tone of the call," one SWAT team veteran says. "Everybody needs to be very calm, cool, clear, and concise. If you're on your way to a call and the officer already there is screaming over the radio, it tends to get you really jacked up. The same thing with the dispatcher—if she's sounding a bit panicky, that panic and sense of urgency gets communicated to you, too. I always make a conscious effort to sound calm on the radio because it is very important for the other officers on the channel to understand what I am telling them."

High-Risk Warrants

A high-risk arrest or search warrant is a type of *deliberate* mission that sometimes has the luxury of time to prepare and plan. These

Information from the observer teams is collected and distilled into diagrams back at the CP.

missions are launched against suspected drug laboratories, known violent prior offenders, or people who are known to be heavily armed. Basically, a high- risk warrant is one where everybody knows, going in, that there is likely to be a fight—and that, without special precautions, somebody is going to get hurt.

This mission will start in a briefing room in the headquarters building. The team will plan the raid. For a deliberate operation of this type, planning begins with the warrant itself. A worksheet is prepared specifying the kind of action (probation or parole search, for example, or a search or arrest warrant). The suspect or suspects will be identified and described in de-

During the slow, progressive, deliberate assault on a lone gunman, three members of the team conduct a whispered conference.

tail, including tattoos, normal clothing, and with photographs normally attached. If vehicles are involved in any way, they too are identified and described.

Generally the location is under police surveillance for some time before the planning, and this provides information important to the operators. Are there guard dogs to deal with? Children? Chemicals, like ether, used in drug manufacture and explosively flammable? Weapons available to the suspects?

During the briefing, the operational details are defined: the date and time of the operation, the names of the primary individuals and agencies responsible for the raid, and phone

numbers.

The staging area is identified, along with the target locations, including addresses and physical descriptions. Again photos will normally be attached. So will a floor plan of the target location, if possible, and sometimes—when they are available—photos of the interior.

The people on the team are specified: supervisor or commander, the 844PC officer, the door-kicker; then the names of the people on the front entry team, the arrest team, and the team that will come in through the back door. The "finder"—the officer specifically tasked with identifying and capturing the suspect—is identified.

Specialized equipment is identified, listed, and defined on a worksheet: raid jackets, body armor, radios, flashlights, goggles, dogs.

Often there will be a need for specialized personnel: a female officer if female suspects are involved; someone from the local child protective services agency if there will be children who will need to be taken to a shelter while their parents go to jail; an animal control officer to deal with pit bulls; a transport vehicle to collect the crowd of arrestees.

The team will also make sure the communications center knows what's happening before all the citizen calls start coming in on the 911 line. The fire department, ambulance service, and nearby agencies may all need to be advised—along with the on-call district attorney and judge who will be hearing the preliminary proceedings against the people arrested.

Finally, the time and location of the pre-operation briefing will be indicated, along with the radio channel the raid units will use.

Right on schedule, all the players will assemble at the appointed place and time. This will normally be a conference room in the police department headquarters, a room that offers secure privacy, convenience, and access to all the intelligence resources of the department's files and experts. The briefing, usually led by the team leader and commander, is a step-by-step discussion of the op, followed by questions and answers. The team commander will probably remind everybody about any relevant SOPs and department rules and regulations that apply, and then it's show time.

The players, with gear and wearing tactical attire, move to their assigned vehicles and relocate to a site near the location. There they may be briefed again. The team moves to the location, usually a residence, in a convoy of unmarked vehicles called a caravan, and—on cue—bail out of the vehicles and form a "snake" to make entry.

Emergency Operations

An emergency operation will develop very differently than a deliberate op, and it will (surprisingly) go much slower. The shift of responsibility from the initial incident commander to

In the protected lee of the team's dedicated tank (a recycled armored bank car), an assault team forms a "snake," ready for the command to move to the position of last cover and concealment (LCC) alongside the building.

47

the SWAT team commander is a critical moment in the operation. The hand-off is a formal event between the two commanders, and once completed, the two teams trade places.

The patrol officers who've been securing the scene are withdrawn, but don't get to go home; instead, they are redeployed to form an outer perimeter. They will insulate the SWAT team and their work from the hordes of curious onlookers, the media, and all other distractions.

The sniper/observer teams will crawl, wiggle, and sneak into positions around the problem. These two-officer teams are expert at moving invisibly and watching undetectably. Their mission is crucial during this early phase of the operation. Using all kinds of cover and concealment, they move into positions where they can watch and record information about the scene. They will use their rifle scope, binoculars, military night vision equipment, and the "Mk I eyeball" to study the layout of the scene, any activity in it, and any detail that could conceivably

Many teams have an armored vehicle of some kind to allow protected movement in the face of an adversary with rifle or pistol. The steel plate on this truck and *the heavy, special glass used for the windows will resist virtually all conventional small-arms bullets.*

have an influence on the conduct of the operation. All the data are recorded in notebooks and any activity is reported by radio back to the CP.

While the sniper/observer teams are snuggling into their "hides," other officers are busy collecting other kinds of information. The building manager will be interviewed to find out about access to the location, and about phone lines, air-conditioning ducts, the floor plan, and doors and windows. The blueprint of the building is requested. The telephone company and utility company are contacted and brought into the operation.

This phase of the operation emphasizes the gathering of intelligence, of any and all pertinent information about the site and the people involved. If the identity of the suspect is known, his or her records are rapidly collected from every available source.

Surveillance specialists will work their way in to the location. Using television and still photo cameras, night vision optics, and special sensors (including tiny microphones and camera lenses that can literally see through walls), the suspects are watched and listened to virtually anywhere they go on the location.

Hostage Negotiator

Throughout this activity, a trained hostage negotiator will be attempting to maintain a dialogue with the suspect. This can be an extremely difficult and frustrating part of police work, but the negotiator, more than any other individual, has the potential for bringing the operation to a successful close (the suspect in custody, the hostages released, nobody injured).

Negotiating with people under these circumstances is dangerous to your mental health. The suspects are normally extremely emotional, inconsistent, and sometimes incomprehensible. It takes incredible tact and self-discipline to maintain contact with these people, but it has to be done.

One technique some negotiators use when they start negotiations is to consider all the hostages already doomed—and then to try to buy back their lives, one at a time. A negotiator may have to listen while a suspect shoots or injures a hostage just to prove she or he means business.

The negotiator will try to keep the suspect on the phone, to wear him or her down, tire the suspect out. Negotiators can collect essential intelligence, probe for weakness, stall for time. The negotiator can also bargain for advantages—one hostage will be sent out for, say, a pizza—or a bulletproof vest. "There are some things we will never negotiate," says one officer. "We will never negotiate weapons for hostages, or hostages for hostages."

Every contact is reported, and every contact helps develop a psychological profile of the suspect. That profile will include previous criminal history, military service history, employment, information about (and from) friends, family, and associates. This takes the efforts of many people making lots of phone calls.

Although the negotiators are an essential element of the team and the program, their needs conflict with those of the rest of the SWAT team. As one team commander says:

"Ideally, we like to have the administrative command post [ACP] and the tactical command post [TCP] separated. Most of the time somebody on our SWAT team will be there first, before the administrative folks like me show up. The first team member defines where the ACP will be, coordinating and consulting the watch commander and the team leader.

"We try to make sure the [TCP] is within the perimeter—to give us some protection from the bad guys. All the bosses respond immediately to the ACP.

"We want the hostage negotiators with us, but separated from us. We want to have access to them, to communicate easily with them, maybe listen in—but we don't want them in the same room with us! They conflict with what we do, and we conflict with what they do.

"Hopefully, as the bosses arrive, they don't even know where the [TCP] is—we simply don't need those kinds of interruptions."

Teamwork and Team Focus

"The most important things about a special ops team are the ways people are *selected* and

After the explosives detonate, the assault team pours through the breech. It is essential, even if fire is received from inside, that the assault continue to get everyone out of the "fatal funnel" at the doorway, where SWAT team members are often hit.

In they go! Each weapon is directed away from team members but is ready to engage the suspects if necessary.

trained for these missions. Experience and training are essential. If something can go wrong, it will. Any one person on the team can defeat the efforts of the rest—as happens all too often," says an officer.

One example of a team member creating a problem on an operation occurred when the Berkeley (California) Police Department responded to a hostage incident in 1990. A lone gunman entered a popular bar one early evening, removed a Mac 10 pistol and a mini Uzi from a briefcase and started shooting. He killed a waitress and wounded others of the approximately 150 patrons, whom he then took hostage. The subject used the bar patrons and furniture to barricade himself, and the siege began.

The Berkeley SWAT team responded, along with all the local news media. The scene was not secured by the patrol division and soon there were television crews providing live reports of the incident The media were allowed to compromise the operation and the gunman had the luxury of watching every move of the police as they responded to his actions.

"When it came time for the hostage rescue mission to be launched, one of the team members, one of the first officers in the snake to assault the position, came close to getting many of the rest of the team killed," an officer from another jurisdiction recalls. "He had been giving out a lot of signs that he wasn't really committed to the mission. He'd been saying things like, 'Tell my wife I love her' and similar clues that he was distracted and that he wasn't thinking about the mission. When it came time for him to confront and control the suspect, he broke—endangering everyone on the team, and the hostages as well. Other members of the entry team successfully engaged the gunman

The MP-5 submachine gun is carried at the ready position, mounted to the shoulder, oriented slightly down, finger off the trigger. This carry position provides good mobility and visibility, but still lets the officer engage almost instantly.

(who took twenty-five hits), despite the failure of this one man, but it was an object lesson for us all. He should have been jerked from the mission at the first sign of a bad attitude. You can't go into an op like that. Everybody has to be able to rely on each other, and their focus has to be 100 percent on the mission."

Rehearsal for the Big Show

Once the team commander is satisfied that a forcible entry will be required, a plan is developed and published within the team. The plan is briefed in detail, assignments are made, and then a curious thing happens—most of the team withdraws from the scene and goes away.

In fact, they go to a school, a large office, or any other place that can be secured, and there they conduct a series of rehearsals. Schools are perfect for this, usually. The floor plan for the location is taped out on the floor of the rehearsal site: doors, windows, obstacles of all kinds. The assault team members shed their heavy gear and begin to walk through their entry.

They will rehearse the assault several times this way, first slowly and then faster. Then they put on some of the equipment they shed earlier, and rehearse some more. Gradually, they replace all the heavy, bulky gear and weapons, until they have been through the moves fifteen or twenty times and are perfectly familiar with every move and can do it at a run—in the dark.

"When police special operations teams are developed and trained, the vast majority of their strategies and tactics are based on a military model," explains Dr. Ron Martinelli. "But the mission statement for law enforcement has one essential difference from that of a military unit; a military operation will always have factored in an 'acceptable casualty rate' for the friendly unit. The only acceptable casualty rate in law enforcement operations is zero. When the Army's Delta, the British Special Air Service (SAS), or the US Navy's SEALs go in to rescue hostages, they are there to do only two things: kill the bad guys and save the good guys. There's no middle ground. But in law en-

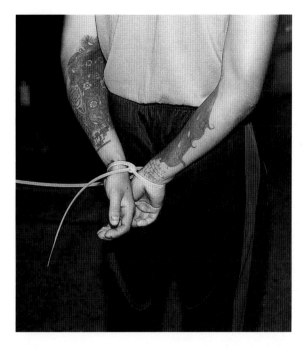

SWAT operations, unlike military ones, are successes only when nobody gets killed or hurt—including the bad guys. This one, a gangster with prison tattoos and a bad attitude, has been collected and cuffed with plastic ties. Now comes the hard part for the officers, the paperwork; as their saying goes, "You catch 'em, you clean 'em."

forcement we have to be concerned about the safety of the officers, the safety of the hostages, and—believe it or not—the safety of the subject we're moving against. Of course there are times when the only alternative is to shoot and kill the subject to save everybody else. That's a lot different from military hostage rescue operations where (as in the Iranian embassy in London takedown by the SAS) the hostage takers are going to all be quickly and efficiently killed once the team assaults the building.

"Law enforcement officers frequently die in the line of duty. These people get killed because of several common reasons: some are not committed to the mission; others are not sufficiently trained, not sufficiently proficient with the tactics and weapons needed to carry out their part of the mission. There is a frequent over-reliance on military tactics—instead of the slower, more deliberate version of the same basic mission that has been developed for law enforcement situations.

"A good police trainer makes sure officers and special units are flexible in their approach to tactics. There are times for explosive, 'door-kick' entries, but a more deliberate, methodical entry will work better most of the time. "

The Fatal Funnel

Entry or assault team tactics are essentially military close-quarter urban combat techniques adapted to civilian situations. Doing your job on an entry team is part art, part science, and all discipline. When an entry is unopposed, when an entry team does everything they are supposed to do, the operation is quick

Although the first officers at the door are called "kickers," few of them attempt to kick in a door; it is a good way to go on disability with foot and knee injuries. Instead, some variation of this ram or other forcible *entry tool is employed. This one is home-brewed, weighs about thirty pounds, and will reliably open most residential doors on the first try.*

and smooth, and nobody gets hurt. From door-kick to cuffing the suspects will often take less than sixty seconds.

But when things go to hell—when the suspects come up shooting, when there are casualties on the entry team, when the intel doesn't match the interior—the quality of team training and operational planning will have a lot to do with the life expectancy of the team, any innocents, and the suspects themselves.

One of the most dangerous moments is that instant when the door flies open and the point-man takes the first step into the unknown. If he takes fire—and stops to return it—the tempo of the assault is ruined, and team casualties are likely to result.

The teams call this the "fatal funnel" because the point-man is both a perfect target, standing there in the door, and is all by himself for an instant. The point-man's reaction to fire will determine how well the op is going to go. In one bungled entry by the San Jose Police Department's MERGE unit, the point-man fumbled the entry and was shot in the head! And this was on a team whose leadership had rejected the Kevlar helmet as too costly.

One officer on that op says, "If you get hit and it isn't too bad, you need to engage the suspect right away; if you are hit significantly, you need to go down and get out of the way so other officers can walk over you, follow up, and neutralize the threat!"

Years ago, in the jungles of Vietnam, the military found that the best way to react to an ambush was to assault right through it, and that's SWAT doctrine, too. Once the assault begins, it needs to flow quickly and deliberately into the structure.

In a normal high-speed raid, each team member should know what his or her route into the building will be and what his or her field of fire and area of responsibility is. Each has a slice of the pie, and each should normally split the slice in half, going right up the middle.

"It is mind-set and commitment," a team captain says. "For those of us that have had the opportunity to do this, when the bad guys start pulling triggers and popping caps, *know* that

This team calls their careful, deliberate movement to the final assault position "stealth to contact." It involves a careful, wary movement into and through a structure, always guarding against possible threats. And one of the most threatening places and most difficult to clear are stairways like this one, where adversaries can pop over the rail and bang away at you, then instantly retreat.

your mind-set has to be established before you go in—or you will never make the commitment to penetrate far enough. You have to have the commitment for the team tactics to work, to solve the problem!"

"When you go into your AOR," a team sergeant says, "and you hear a 'cap busted' (i.e., shot fired) you may want to turn toward that sound to protect yourself. But, when you do that, the whole team is compromised! You can't tell by sound where a shot is coming from inside a room; it is easy to make a mistake. You have to concentrate on your AOR and take care of your assignment. If you start worrying about somebody else's AOR the whole assault falls apart."

Drug Raids

Drug raids pose a set of special problems for police departments, and for that reason many departments use the special skills, training, and equipment of the SWAT teams for this particular mission.

Drug raids are typically conducted against people who are a bit smarter than the common crook, people who are able to plan, organize, and execute operations of their own. People in the drug trade are often awash in cash, and that cash is often used to pay for all sorts of things that can help defeat the police: guns, information, and surveillance equipment.

In addition to the danger posed by a house full of people with guns, raids on drug labs may expose the team to the danger of tremendously toxic chemicals and explosive solvents.

A drug raid has all the problems of a high-risk warrant service mission (high probability of weapons in the house, an inclination toward violence, a mixture of innocent people—including children—in with the bad guys) plus all kinds of acids, explosive vapors, and a good chance that the whole place is full of booby traps.

The entry to a room where suspects are expected is explosive and carefully choreographed, with each officer moving through his or her assigned AOR. The first man breaks left, the second right, and the third is about a tenth of a second away from shooting the photographer.

Well, you better have your hands up and empty when this happens or you're going to have a bad case of heartburn, one that Rolaids can't begin to touch. The final assault depends on speed and shock effect for surprise, and if done correctly it usually works perfectly.

People in the drug trade often have the money for the best, newest, and most advanced radio scanners that let them listen in on police radio traffic. They buy and use the latest surveillance cameras and microphones—and they buy high-quality night vision goggles just as good or better than those of the police. Sophisticated drug houses can be guarded by sophisticated alarm systems, including vibration sensors, thermal sensors, and trip wires.

"We raided a house used by a Hell's Angels dealer in 'crank' [methamphetamine] that produced automatic weapons and a lot of drugs. But the house was booby trapped with 'det' cord that had been rigged around the door; the explosive was rigged to a trip cord about four inches above the floor. Thank God we had intelligence information that warned us about the explosives and booby traps in the house!"

As a result, planning for a drug raid begins

Even during the final phases of the assault, some members of the team will guard and isolate the entry team. In fact, a SWAT operation effectively puts a noose around the criminal and tightens it, slowly and firmly, with plenty of opportunities offered for surrender. Then, if the suspect doesn't cooperate, it is finally jerked tight.

with the collection of as much information as possible. That includes information from inside the house, if possible, through informants. For a variety of reasons, including revenge, plea bargains, and cash, people will provide information on their ex-wife or husband, partner in crime, or brother. Police departments usually have budgets for this kind of information, and

All dressed up with no place to go. The black uniform makes it very difficult for crooks to see, identify, and engage individual officers, particularly in the dark. And the big flashlight on the Uzi makes it rather easy to engage the suspect no matter how dark and dank his hiding hole might be.

it is sometimes a very good investment. The cops call these informants "snitches."

"Even on a low-level threat entry," says one officer, "we always assume the residents have access to weapons. There are very few houses you go into where there aren't weapons, particularly handguns."

Planning includes consideration of the threat level and weapons, number of people to be arrested, number of innocents (including children in the residence), animals present, type of structure, and method of entry

"In these kinds of ops," an officer says, "I tend to go slower rather than faster. Unlike some teams that approach every entry as if it were a hostage rescue, where the element of surprise is so important, I'm more concerned about avoiding mistakes—'dumping' somebody when I shouldn't, for example. I have found that a slower, deliberate, careful entry will get your guy every single time, and nobody gets hurt."

"A common mistake of special ops teams executing drug raids is to focus excessively on seizure of the evidence," says Martinelli. "In my opinion, the prime objective of these operations is *officer safety*. There is no acceptable level of casualties. I am going to take my time going in. I'm going to make sure that I am alive at the end of the op, that everybody on my team is alive at the end of the day. If the dope gets flushed, that's too bad. I'm not there for the dope, I'm there for the 'fun'—to do the operation. There are a lot of sophisticated weapons out there, and I don't want to be on the receiving end of any of them.

"When we conduct these ops it really pays to do your 'front' work, your planning and preparation—your collection of intelligence,— really carefully. If you do that, you don't have to do a lot of 'back' work—the things that you are forced to do when things go sour.

"It pays to have all your heavy firepower up front. You put your most proficient entry people up front, along with your best, most proficient weapons people, your best 'door-kicker' with all the right entry tools. You need to have good intelligence—to know just what kind of door you'll be going through, whether the place is fortified or not.

"When you go in, either fast or slow, the object is to confuse the people in the place with shock and surprise to neutralize them, to put them down in a hurry, shouting at them and keeping them disoriented and unable to respond against us."

Mobilizing for an Assault

Once the team has been notified, its members report to the TCP, the tactical command post. The TCP will be isolated, but near the ACP, the administrative command post, where the news media and all the nontactical support part of the operation is staged and managed.

"We frequently compromise our own security, "said one officer," by talking too much on the radio, by giving out too many clues about what we are doing. I have never been in a drug house that didn't have at least one scanner in the house and one guy had three, with a detailed log going back three months. He had scanners with all the exotic channels and was keeping careful track of our callsigns and activity."

From the TCP the team will move to the FUP, the form-up position that will be located somewhere within the outer perimeter, with the patrol division providing basic security. The team leader will get up in front of the group and say, "Okay, here's the situation . . . We will mobilize immediately. . . I need three 'wolf pack' teams, one evac team, two 'sierra' teams. . ." and the team will be officially mobilized. The team puts together the operation order immediately, within the relative quiet and security of the FUP.

After briefing and a final check of personnel and equipment, the team will move to the LCC position, the last cover and concealment, before the assault. This is the last safe place for the team, a jumping off point for the assault and a place to regroup or reform in case of disaster. The actual assault will not normally launch from here, but from an even closer position at the more exposed FAP, the final assault

This officer is a guard at San Francisco's main jail facility, a facility with its own specialized need for special operations skills, training, and equipment. When prisoners acquire guns and hostages—which they do, in spite of everything—many facilities have their own integral SWAT teams to resolve the situation. These officers are practicing building-clearing techniques borrowed from the military and modified for civil applications like this.

position.

"Wolf pack 1, move to FAP," might be the next call from the team commander, moving the entry team up to the very edge of the residence. The teams will slither forward, as silently and precisely as possible. The FAP can be right outside the front door, or right around the corner from the subject. When the assault teams are all in position, the tactical channel announces, "Wolf pack 1 in position. Wolf pack 2 in position. Wolf pack 3 in position," as each team reports in to C2.

"Confirm at FAP," the C2 will radio, and each team responds in sequence, "Wolf pack 1, confirm we are at FAP." Once all the teams are confirmed in position, the assault is ready to go.

Setting up the CP and comparing notes, the SWAT team commander and sergeants conspire early in an event.

Making Entry

When it comes time to drop in on the residence, the entry team will be composed of several subunits. In the lead will be the door-kickers with their rams, pry-bars, and—occasionally—explosives. They are part of the unit that forces entry. They are responsible for opening the structure and securing it, making sure nobody pops out of the woodwork with a shotgun to make things complicated for the visitors. The entry team, if they are proficient, will quickly clear each room, search every hidden space, and control every person in the residence. It is a very difficult job to do well because it is done amid great noise, emotional distress of the residents, and because the entry team can't easily determine who is, and who isn't, a threat;

women holding babies sometimes produce pistols and try to kill members of entry teams. Sometimes they succeed.

Right behind the entry team, toward the end of the "snake," is the arrest team, the officers who will sort out the bad guys from the good, the innocents from the suspects. As the entry team moves through the residence, securing it, the arrest team follows, secures the people, room by room. Everybody will probably be "proned-out" or on their knees within a few seconds of the entry team's appearance, and in handcuffs shortly thereafter.

"Making entrance and clearing a residence are very difficult problems," says one veteran officer. "There are a million places to hide—in closets, under beds, behind television sets. And the people hiding can be little kids, innocent wives, and family members. You have to carefully consider the environment you are going into. Is it dark or bright in there? Are the people you encounter armed or unarmed; if armed, is it some innocent trying to protect their home? You have to sort out the good guys from the bad guys under the most difficult of circumstances."

"Most of the houses that I have raided looked like they had already been burglarized. And some of the houses are *full* of people—ten or twelve people living in a tiny little house."

Snipers

The snipers can be ordered to launch the assault with carefully coordinated shots. For example, when the entry teams are all lined up at the entry points, the snipers may be told to shoot the suspects, and the shots cue everybody to go.

Since snipers so often have to shoot into plate glass or automobile windows, deflection of the first shot has to be anticipated. One sniper might break the glass to allow another sniper to have a clear shot. Both will attempt to "double tap," to put a second bullet on top of the first, for insurance. As soon as the snipers fire, though, the radio will come alive with first the snipers' radio call, "Shot away! Shot away! Shot away!" That will normally prompt the commander to issue the execute order, "GO! GO! GO!"

"We are support for the entry teams," a sniper says. "The main thing we do isn't shooting, it is observing the target and reporting as the assault team moves up. We provide information and scouting. We cover the 'wolf pack' teams and protect them as they move up from LCC to the FAP. If we see the subject come out and discover the team moving up, we will take him out right then and there, but we will also notify everybody. If we can take the guy out before the teams have to make an entry, we will—it is dangerous as hell to make one of these assaults. But our mission is basically to support the entry teams.

"While we operate as six, twelve, or eigh-

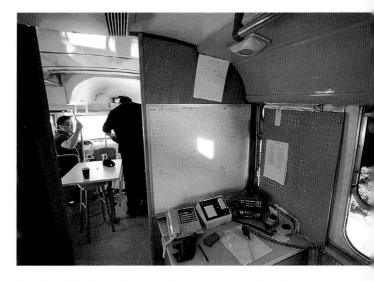

Interior, CP. There is normally a separate station for each specialist, with telephones, chalkboards, radios, and supplies. These vehicles are normally converted versions of large mobile homes or old buses.

teen officers on the SWAT team, we really operate as two officers inside the AO [Area of operations]. We use the same 'buddy' system that the SEALs and Special Forces have been using for years. If you can't work as a two-officer pair, you're out of here. And you have to work with anybody on the team, under stress."

Point-man

The first officer in the door, the head of the "snake," is designated the point-man. The point-man is typically the first to fire, and the first to get shot at. This officer, unlike the ones who follow, typically can engage anybody in the room, a full 360-degree angle of responsibility. If somebody pops out from behind the front door with a shotgun, the point-man is supposed to get him or her if that person is a threat to the team. One point-man explains, "If you're on point, you're responsible for the first immediate threat anywhere within 360 degrees, from four to eight feet from the door. Even if you're supposed to 'hook right'—if there's somebody standing three feet from the door on the left you've got to sense that because it is an immediate threat to the team."

The point-man does the primary search as the team penetrates into the building. He or she has to stay low because his buddy, the "cover-man," will be shooting past and over at threats as the point pulls the team forward. In really massive raids, such as hostage rescue missions, ten or twenty rooms might get hit simultaneously—with ten or twenty point-men leading the way into each. For an operation like the planned assault on the Branch Davidian compound in Waco, Texas, there were *120* point-men, one for each of the small assigned areas-of-responsibility, which the original assault team was planning to hit all at once.

Cover-man or Post-man

The point-man is the first officer into the AOR, protected by either the cover- or post-man. As the point-man enters the AOR, moving forward into it, he or she is quite vulnerable to flank attacks that can come from dozens of places in any home. So while the point moves forward, the cover-man and post-man guard against threats from his "flanking unknown," the unsecured area on the point-officer's side and rear. The post-man assumes a stationary position behind the threshold of a door, the corner of a wall, or behind any other protection the building offers. It works almost anywhere—a room, a parking lot, an office building, a warehouse.

"If I see my point-man has his weapon pointing to the right, as we go into a room," one team member explains, "I scan the area to the left. As he checks out the unknowns, I move up with him to cover the unknowns on the other side of our AOR."

A good team conducting a stealth-to-contact operation moves quickly through the AORs with a fluid grace, and often in virtual silence. Using hand and arm signals, the teams can bound forward, from covered position to covered position. Post-men slide into positions at the corners of hallways, while the point-men move forward to clear the hallway, then stop to

evaluate and bring up the cover element for the next bound. The point-men use hand and arm signals to describe danger areas, and to ask for cover.

It is quite easy for the point-officer to bypass a secondary area of threat in the rush of an assault, but it is essential that areas of the room that could hold hidden suspects—behind televisions, under beds, behind doors, in closets—get covered (first), then cleared (second) in a methodical, thorough, and prompt way. Sometimes, in the excitement of the raid, untrained officers or badly prepared teams breeze right through a residence, call "all clear," and break for coffee and doughnuts. That kind of over-confidence can and regularly does get officers killed. One officer, from a jurisdiction whose identity will remain confidential, reports:

"I have been on operations where things have been done too quickly and mistakes have happened. For example, on one op we had a house full of Vietnamese 211 [robbery] suspects. Our department's Intelligence unit went in first to clear the house while my guys took the inner perimeter. The intel guys must have gotten carried away, because they weren't even supposed to go in the place—they just ran right past us. Then their leader came out and said 'The house is clear!'" Then we went in . . . and the second room I entered had a very *lumpy* mattress on the floor, with something clearly under it. When I turned it over there was a guy with a .44 magnum pistol in his hand. I stepped on the wrist of the hand with the gun and shoved my pistol into his head until the situation was resolved. That's the kind of thing that happens when you go too fast."

Pickup-man

The last member of the entry team is the "cleanup" member of the group, and this job often falls to the team leader. The assignment goes by a variety of names, depending on the department: hands-on man, equipment-man, and gun-bearer are common terms for the same job. A team might have ten point-men, five post-men, and one pickup member, or perhaps

An armored car pulls up to the loading dock of the building where hostages have been taken. One of the two gunmen has been wounded and staggers out.

He's collected by several members of the team, one of whom uses a ballistic shield to provide some heavy, fairly mobile armor.

five of each—it just depends on the mission and the desires of the team leaders and operation planners.

The pickup member of the team looks for things the others may have missed—a room that, for whatever reason, has been missed. Another role is to secure suspects, to do the "hands-on" work required to cuff people discovered by the point-men. And, finally, the pickup-man steps in for any of the others if one of them gets shot, to keep the operation moving ahead.

The pickup-man's weapons are the same as the others—preferably a shoulder weapon like an MP5 or a shotgun, with a sling, but possibly just a handgun. This player will also carry any specialized equipment that is appropriate for the mission—like lots of handcuffs, or nylon ties, when multiple suspects are expected.

Medic

The role of the team medic varies, but preferably this member will be stationed at the LCC, ready to go in if somebody gets hit. Medics are particularly valuable in incidents where a scene is too insecure for conventional paramedics or ambulance personnel, a fairly common problem. When one or more of the team goes down on an op, the medic is sup-

Within two or three seconds, the suspect is swept up, cuffed, and secured in the back of the vehicle. He'll be extracted at the CP for preliminary medical treat-ment—and a heart-to-heart chat with the intel team, if possible.

posed to be working on the injured officer even while bullets may be flying in adjacent rooms. And, since the medic is fully qualified and equipped as a member of the team, he or she can engage suspects if required.

Rear Guard

It is amazing how people can pop up from the darndest places, like from behind doors, to take a pop at your backside when you are least expecting it. The rear guard, also frequently called the "tail gunner," is brought along to make such a shot more difficult. One rear guard explains:

"When you are outside, moving through the weeds, your rear guard covers your 'six-o'clock' position, to make sure nobody moves up behind you. Inside a building, the rear guard covers areas you've bypassed or have already cleared—plus doorways and hallways you might not have gotten to yet. Basically, I'm there to cover your back."

Surveillance

SWAT missions succeed or fail on the quality of the information used to plan and execute them. Some of that information is acquired before the op begins, but a lot of it is gathered after the team shows up at the location of the incident, particularly in hostage rescues and barricaded suspect operations.

The surveillance specialist's bag of high-tech tricks can be pretty amazing: "spike mikes" that can be inserted into walls and transducer mikes that can record through concrete walls. These allow the intel specialists to monitor anything said in a room and provide important information about the state of mind of the people inside.

Miniature television cameras can be set up to cover many areas of a location. These cameras allow team members to monitor, from a distance, a room, hall, courtyard, or other danger area, and provide advance warning when things start to go bad. Other television cameras can be inserted into a crawl space before an officer climbs in—just in case there is a bad guy or a booby trap hidden inside. There are video systems that can provide views from under doors, through the keyhole, and *through* the door.

Most teams now use little video still cameras, which have been marketed as a kind of electronic alternative to the traditional Polaroid "instant" picture technology. Using a small data disk similar to those used in computers, this little camera can record about ten still pictures of fairly low resolution, which can then be viewed on a conventional television. "These images are great for planning," one intel specialist says. "We can make a videotape record of the pictures, and we can transmit it to other locations. But it is a fixed-focal length system—what you see is what you get. You can't zoom in on something to pick out a detail, but it's auto-everything, and anybody can use it."

Most teams also have and use conventional photography systems, with unconventionally long telephoto lenses—800mm, for example—that can provide extremely detailed imagery.

These systems are used when time permits the film to be processed and returned to the team for planning.

Raid Tactics

SWAT movement techniques are based very much on the lessons learned from the military's careful development of urban combat skills during and since World War II. There are differences, of course, but there is also a lot of cross-training between teams and their counterparts in the Marine Corps, Army, and occasionally with military special operations forces—Delta, the Navy's SEALs, and the Army's Rangers and Green Berets. SWAT teams regularly take advantage of the special facilities the military has developed for practicing such skills; these are sometimes called "tire houses" because they are built from old tires to absorb bullets.

One of the team's basic movement techniques is a version of a technique the Army and Marines call "bounding overwatch." As used by SWAT units, this technique involves two officers alternating between point and cover positions. The officer on point will move forward, staying at a low crouch, while the other officer provides cover from a doorway or a corner. When the point-man reaches cover—another door or corner—he signals the other officer forward and they trade roles; the officer on point now becomes the cover-man, and assumes a good firing position. The cover-man passes him, becoming the point, moves deeper into the building, and then takes up a firing position behind suitable cover. It is a technique that works while advancing or retreating.

Large, complicated structures like residences require the team to enter and penetrate rooms in progressive stages, but there will be rooms and spaces that don't need to actually be entered—like a bedroom or other space that might typically be only ten feet on a side. If there aren't hiding spaces in the room, it can be covered from the door by two officers, one on each side of the door, each covering an AOR. These AORs overlap. And, since the longest shot either would have to make is only about

In some ways, the outcome of SWAT operations is determined by the person who initiates the action. An operation can end peacefully or violently, but one way or another the cops are going to prevail and the crooks are going to lose. How bad the crooks lose is usually up to the crook. This one (in a training exercise using an officer as an actor) has elected to kill himself.

twelve feet, there isn't a need to enter the room. A team sergeant says, "We aren't going to penetrate small rooms if we don't have to. If we are going to shoot, we will fire from the door, from a position of cover."

Rally points are predetermined locations where the team regroups, either during an entry (perhaps if something goes wrong and the plan is overcome by events) or after the structure is completely cleared. These are specified in the pre-operation briefing, when the team leader says something like, " . . . Wolf pack 1 will penetrate the hallway and these two rooms; the rally point will be the doorway to the first room." Then, to collect all the players after the show, the briefer might say, "Wolf pack 1, at the termination of the incident, we want you to rally on the front lawn."

Sometimes a two-officer buddy team will need to get back together; then one officer will tell the other officer—either verbally or by using hand signals—to rally at a specific location. These buddy-team rally points can be discussed and agreed on during the planning phase of the mission, or even as the mission goes down; one might say, "If we get into a problem, let's hook up *here.*"

Drug Raid

Drug raids are a stock-in-trade mission for many teams, deliberate operations that allow plenty of planning and the development of good intel. One officer tells what it's like to prepare these raids:

"One of our specialties is dealing with fortified 'crack' houses. Over the course of thirteen weeks we trained to take down a particularly difficult one. There was heavy dealing from the residence, and an earlier attempt to raid it failed. This time we concentrated on surveillance, from the air as well as from vans, and trained hard to make the entry.

"When we started training, it took two minutes for the SWAT team just to get deployed out of the vehicles. When the raid went down, after all those weeks of training, we deployed, made entry, arrested the bad guys, and had the evidence in hand in under two minutes, even with a major communications gear breakdown! Nobody got hurt, good guys or bad guys, and we got what we came for. That shows you what good training will do."

Berkeley Mission Postmortem Conference

After major operations, particularly in which there are hostages and fatalities, the unit involved will often conduct a kind of seminar on the lessons learned from the experience, and they will share that information with members of other teams. That's a rather brave thing to do because there are always mistakes ,and they can be embarrassing. When things go wrong on a SWAT op, they tend to go *real* bad. But even the Berkeley officers stood up in front of their peers to talk about their difficult operation against the guy in the bar.

The Berkeley team described and discussed

the problems they identified with the operation. First, they hadn't been prepared to use a sniper to shoot through the thick glass windows when the opportunity presented itself. Second, television news teams were able to cover the activity outside the location—and the subject was able to watch these reports.

In the case of the Berkeley operation, it was revealed at the post-op conference that when it came time for the team to move on the hostage taker, the team member who had exhibited reservations had the opportunity to shoot the subject—but failed to fire. Two other members of the team had to get around their team member in order to shoot. The subject was hit twenty-five times, despite the barricades and hostages.

Waco and the Branch Davidians

Waco was another operation reviewed in post-operation seminars for the enlightenment of the profession. It was embarrassing for some of the participants, but it revealed that the real mistakes weren't so much tactical, as they were problems of command and control.

The siege and final assault of the Waco compound where David Koresh and his followers met their fiery end in May 1993 was, in some ways at least, a textbook example of how *not* to execute a raid. According to one law enforcement consultant who attended the after-action review seminar, the operation was badly flawed.

"Waco is an excellent example of how *not* to do an op. For example, people were wondering how the news media found out about the original assault; the media knew because ATF *told* them about it, in an effort to get good coverage and, indirectly, to help get additional funding in the next budget. The media, inadvertently, helped tip off the people in the compound.

"Then, the Federal agents just didn't have the training or resources to execute the op. The FBI are people with degrees in business, history, and maybe economics—and who don't know anything about law enforcement, crooks, or weapons. They didn't understand the people they were operating against, and they didn't have to do the raid.

"The feds had an agent inside the compound who reported on the training and weapons, and he reported that the people inside the compound knew that the feds were staging for the raid. I can't tell you who or how they knew, but forty-five minutes before the raid went down, the Branch Davidians knew the raid was coming, and they were preparing for it. The feds were advised of this, and could have—should have—called it off right there. They chose not to.

"The feds failed to take into account the psychological profile of this group, how paranoid they were and what they were prepared to do. Then, over the course of the fifty-two day siege, the Federal agents continued to do things that fed directly into the paranoia of the group, reinforcing the behavior they wanted to defeat.

Dead or alive, the suspect will be handcuffed, secured, and searched. In an operation like this one, where the suspect appears to be dead, the final phase will proceed with glacial slowness. There is no need to take chances now, particularly with a corpse that might only be playing possum.

SWAT Teams have all sorts of high-tech equipment at their disposal. This officer carries a portable shield that provides excellent protection from gun fire.

They used military style 'psyops' to try to keep them off balance, without sleep, and wear them down; instead, it did the opposite, confirming what Koresh had been telling the followers about the government, that the agents on the outside were indeed agents of the devil. It only increased the resolve of the followers to resist, suicidally as it turned out.

"The Army's Delta Force was there, almost from the beginning, along with the FBI's hostage rescue team [HRT]. The operation was pushed by the Clinton Administration and Attorney General Janet Reno, partially because of poor information, and partly because the costs of the siege were so high. The FBI had only two HRTs for the whole country, both of which were bogged down with this operation, and the Department of Justice was afraid they'd be needed for something else. In my opinion, they could have just built a wall around the place and made it into a prison. Everything they did made the situation worse. The total loss of life was six federal agents plus the eighty-five Davidians.

"I can't tell you what happened between Delta and the FBI, but there was a problem, and the FBI was told to do the op on their own. And, the decision was made to not use Delta [the premier US counterterrorist and hostage rescue organization] because of its military nature.

"Finally, the decision to use CS gas [the standard type of tear gas] as a chemical agent was another problem. By poking a lot of holes in the walls of the compound to insert the gas, they let the wind come along and disperse it. The gas had a very limited effect, reduced further because there were many gas masks in the compound. Instead of CS, which takes several seconds to have an effect under the best of conditions, they should have used OC pepper spray, an agent that produces instant blindness and respiratory distress.

"It was a classic case of an operation that went totally sour: negotiations that were totally screwed up, poor assessment of the people, improper staging, bad containment, wrong choice of munitions.

"Doing your front work in this kind of case is really important, and the ATF and FBI didn't seem to understand the group dynamics of cults. The strength of these extremist groups is also their weakness; in this case that was David Koresh. If they had removed David Koresh from the picture prior to the day of the raid it would have been a lot easier to get people to negotiate and fall in line. And David Koresh left the compound every day—sometimes more than once—to shop in town, eat in restaurants. He could have been arrested then by a six- or eight-man arrest team."

One caution, though, on post-operation missions and the tendency to criticize operations after the fact: unless you were there, you don't know all the constraints. It is unfair to make too many judgments about these things unless you were a "player" on the team that conducted the op.

Chapter 3

Close Quarters Combat

Anatomy of an incident

At 1333 hours on a pleasant Thursday afternoon the Sacramento, California, emergency dispatch center receives a 911 call from The Good Guys electronics store at 7020 Stockton Boulevard.

"Nine one one, emergency," answers the dispatcher. "What's your emergency?"

"There's somebody in our store shooting a gun," the voice says. He sounds pretty calm, considering.

"A gun?" asks the dispatcher, somewhat incredulous. "Where's your store?"

A supervisor takes over the call, quickly asking for details: "Are these guys white, black, or Chicano?"

"I have no idea," is the reply. She tries to question him further but he declines. "I gotta go!"

"NO! Stay on the phone with me! If you have to leave, don't hang up, okay? Just drop it!" The line goes dead.

While the supervisor is trying to get information a "two-eleven in progress, shots fired" call is broadcast over the Sacramento Police Department primary communication channel. Within two minutes the first of a huge number

An entry team at last cover and concealment. The weapons carried are were selected for the specific assignment, as well as personal preference: a mixture of shotguns, submachine guns, pistols, and the CAR-15 rifle.

of police cars and motorcycles descend on the scene.

Inside the store are forty-one patrons and staff, plus four Vietnamese men who have taken them all hostage. The four are all immigrants, including three brothers, Lo, Pham, and Long Nguyen, and Cong Tran, all of whom have had trouble with the law, and with school, and who have never held a job. All claim to be affiliated with a notorious street gang, the Oriental Boys, a group long identified by the Sacramento gang task force as active in extortion and violence within the immigrant community. They are armed with a .45cal pistol, two 9mm pistols, and one shotgun.

They round up the patrons and staff and discover one salesman, Al Bodar, hiding. For this, the gunmen tell Bodar that he will be the first to die, and for the next eight and a half hours he will be frequently reminded of the threat.

At first, both the hostages inside and the police outside of the store think the situation is the result of a botched robbery, but the intruders don't seem particularly interested in money. As the dispatcher and then the hostage negotiator, Sgt. Jerry Gomez of the Sacramento County Sheriff's Department, talk to the men, it appears they are really after notoriety. Gomez starts negotiations by assuming a best-case scenario.

"Hello," he begins. "I'm Sergeant Gomez from the Sacramento Sheriff's Department. I understand you want to give up."

Sgt. Linda Shepherd engages targets during a close quarter combat drill with the H&K MP-5 subma- *chine gun. The MP-5 has quickly become a favorite weapon in SWAT teams around the country.*

"Give up?" says the suspect on the phone. "No, we don't want to give up! We want to *trade!*"

Gomez tries to talk with one of the men on the phone to find out just what they are interested in trading, but does not have much luck; the language barrier makes the effort very difficult. Then one demand after another is issued by the leader of the group. Sergeant Gomez struggles to understand the man on the phone,

who talks fast and doesn't make a lot of sense. Plus, there is a lot of noise and confusion in the background. Finally, Gomez asks, "Has anybody been shot in there?"

"No!"

"The store is surrounded," Gomez tells them.

"I know that!"

"You're not going to be able to get out of there with the gun."

"I KNOW THAT, MAN!"

"So what is it that you want?"

What they want, to start with, is one bulletproof vest—they will trade one hostage for one vest, says the man on the phone. Then he starts demanding a weapon but can't clearly explain what he wants. Gomez is genuinely confused, but the suspect accuses him of lying.

Finally, one bulletproof vest is sent in with Sgt. Bob Lyons who strips to his underwear to show that he's not armed. At 1452 hours, one of the hostages, Jacquie Arrequn, is released with her son and another child.

1505 hours: All law enforcement vehicles are pulled back from the entrance to the store; Sacramento Special Enforcement Detail (SED) assumes control of the incident from the patrol division, sets up its perimeter, and the second phase of the operation begins.

Out of sight of the gunmen, SED surveillance specialists bore a tiny hole through one wall and install a pinhole video camera to provide a view into much of the front of the store. Although the hole is only about a quarter of an inch across and the lens is flush with the wall, the camera provides "real time" coverage of events that the gunmen believe to be unobserved. A tiny spike mike is also installed, allowing the SED team to listen in on everything in the store.

1530 hours: The hostage takers seem almost incoherent and illogical. They want $4 million in cash; they want to be flown to Thailand so they can kill Viet Cong; they want forty thousand-year-old ginger plants; they want tea brewed from ten of the ginger plants and delivered to them in the store. Their demands are impossible to meet and are constantly being modified. A new negotiating team, the SED's Critical Incident Negotiating Team operating out of the CP at the scene, take over negotiations from Gomez, who is still downtown at the dispatch center.

The suspect on the phone won't give his name but asks the negotiator to call him "Thailand." He explains his role in the incident, "I want to take the money and weapons and go back to Thailand and kill VC!"

1540 hours: The SED sniper/observer teams report a shot fired inside the address. It turns out to be the gunmen testing the bulletproof vest.

During the afternoon a Buddhist priest and the mother of three of the gunmen are brought in to try to talk to the gunmen, but they are all rebuffed by the young men.

1737 hours: One adult female hostage and three children are released.

1800 hours: Bystanders and media congregate around the shopping center. Local television stations begin live coverage of the incident.

The hostage negotiator and the gunman calling himself "Thailand" negotiate something approximating a deal. It falls apart, and Thailand hands the phone over to another member of the group who identifies himself as "One."

"I was talking to Thailand, and I thought we had worked out an agreement," the negotiator says. "I *guaranteed* that all you guys would not get hurt, the police will not hurt you, you can keep your vests in jail . . . and he said you were going to send out all the hostages. I thought we had a good agreement—and now he says you don't want to do that. Why?"

"We don't *want* to!"

"Why? What are you going to do?"

"We want three bulletproofs," One says. "And you better have them here in thirty minutes."

"Let me ask you this . . . "

"No! Three bulletproofs! In thirty minutes!"

"Why don't you just come out?"

"No—you're not demanding us [sic], we're demanding YOU! We're the ones that got the guns in here. We want three bulletproofs, we don't care how you get it, within thirty minutes. You want to see what happens—wait thirty-one minutes."

"What happens then?"

"We'll blow everybody up!"

Later, the police prepare to deliver three vests, one at a time, in exchange for one or more hostages for each vest. One of the hostages gets on the phone with the demand. "Three people, three vests," says the hostage to the negotiator.

"One at a time," the negotiator replies, and it is passed on to One.

"LISTEN UP AND LISTEN GOOD," screams One over the phone, "Get us those damn bulletproofs or there will be one dead person—one of those two standing by the door!"

1900 hours: With fading daylight, observers can now see large numbers of hostages arrayed at the front of the store as a sort of human shield.

1725 hours: The gunmen begin binding the hostages with speaker wire.

1950 hours: A seven-man entry team work their way into the ceiling of the store through a crawl space from an adjacent business. Using floor plans supplied by the building owners, the team drops into a storage room at the back of the store, prepared to make a hasty assault if ordered to by the team commander.

2027 hours: A male hostage is released to deliver another impossible demand; the gunmen want more vests but aren't willing to bargain for them.

During the evening one of the women hostages is escorted to the bathroom by one of the gunmen while the seven-member assault team observes from their hiding place. Later she is brought back again, this time by two of the suspects, while the assault team ponders whether to take them out or not; the decision is to hold tight and stay in hiding.

The gunmen select one of the hostages, Sean McIntyre, and shoot him in the thigh to dramatize their demands. "Want me to shoot another?" One taunts the negotiator. "Make me mad and I'll shoot another person!"

2054 hours: McIntyre is brought out for the TV cameras and sent out the door to deliver a message to the assembled reporters: "They want three bulletproof jackets," he says, "a helicopter, and firearms. They already shot me. That's all I have to say."

2145 hours: After negotiating the release of nine more hostages for a second vest, a vest is delivered to the door. Before any hostages are released, however, one man collapses and is shot in the leg by one of the gunmen, who adds

that the next shot will be in his chest and then another to his head. Negotiations are suspended.

2150 hours: One of the gunmen begins threatening the hostages, sometimes holding a pistol to their heads. He appears excited, and the incident command group believes the hostages may soon be executed.

"I think I can get a shot," one of the snipers transmits over the radio.

The phone line from inside seems unattended. "Pick up the phone, somebody," calls the negotiator, over and over, without effect. The gunmen have moved to the front of the store to retrieve the vests. Over the phone line the negotiator can hear distant conversation and the sounds of movement, just as he has heard for many hours.

2151 hours: The three vests are delivered to the door. One of the hostages, Priscilla Alverez, is sent out to retrieve one. She is bound with wire and tethered to prevent escape. As she reaches for the vest, one of the snipers fires a bullet at the gunman standing by the door. The shot was the signal to initiate the SED's hasty assault.

Over the phone line the negotiator hears the *boom* as the shot is fired and strikes a millisecond later. Instead of hitting the gunman squarely in the crosshairs, the bullet hits the glass of the front door—swinging closed at just the worst possible instant. The glass shatters and some of the fragments strike the gunman in the face; a stun grenade is tossed toward the door but detonates just outside with minimal effect. The sound of the shot is followed by a long, loud "AHHHHHH!" from someone near the phone, probably (from the sound of the voice) Thailand, who has just taken a face full of crumbled glass instead of a bullet to the head. Then: *bam! bam! bam! bam! bam! bam!! bam!! bam!! bam!! bam!! bam!! bam!! bam!* The gunman by the door fires thirteen shots, as quickly as he can pull the trigger, as he walks down the line of bound hostages, shooting at the head of each.

The burglar alarm bell begins to ring. There is screaming, crying, and yelling from the hostages, and the gunmen.

There is a lull in the firing for three or four seconds. The only sound the negotiator hears is of someone crying. Then the shooting begins again: two shots as an SED team member outside takes out the gunman who has just shot the hostages. Then another lull—longer this time; the entry team assaults through the store, moving 125 feet from the storage room to the gunmen. The unit splits into two elements, moves quickly and silently toward the sound of the shooting. Then more firing, this time from the SED assault team. Shots are exchanged for ten seconds.

"One bad guy! One bad guy down!" a deputy yells.

"There's a bad guy there!" screams one of the hostages, pointing out one of the men in hiding.

"Hands up! Get your hands up! Get 'em up! Get 'em up!" Then: *bam! bam! bam! bam! bam! bam!* a one second pause, then *bam! bam! bam!*

"HE'S A BAD GUY! HE'S A BAD GUY!" hostages yell to the SED team, pointing out one of the gangsters.

The gunmen try to escape and evade. One by one they are hunted down, ordered to surrender, then shot as little flurries of gunfire are exchanged. The last shot is fired exactly 183 seconds after the first.

As each is shot they are secured; dead or alive, their hands are cuffed behind their backs. Their weapons are kicked out of range, then retrieved; three of the four are dead at the scene, the fourth survives to be taken into custody. "We have four bad guys!" the assault team leader transmits. The assault phase of the operation is over.

Aftermath: five are dead, three gunmen and two hostages. Eight hostages have been shot by the gunmen and the fourth gunman—to the quiet regret of the assembled law enforcement personnel—survives.

The family of one of the dead hostages is furious—with the police—whom they hold accountable for all the killing. They demand the resignation of the county sheriff, Glen Craig: "He killed my brother," one of the family mem-

The assault element "snake" begins to move toward its prey, a gunman with hostages in a heavily fortified office deep inside a post office building.

75

Waiting for the "kickers" to breach the door; this can be done with explosives, a sledge hammer, or (in this case) with the keys.

bers says, even though the brother was the gunman at the front of the store who fired the thirteen shots at the hostages.

The parents of the three gunmen who were brothers thought of their sons as good kids despite their problems with school and prior encounters with the juvenile justice system. According to their parents, the boys were good, church-going sons who said they were going fishing that day. Their mother, Sao Thi, also blamed the police for the carnage. Despite having been given the opportunity to talk to her sons—they would not talk to her—she said, "If they had let me talk to my son, I could have talked him out of it."

Lessons Learned

The above incident, and hundreds of others, teach people in law enforcement that sometimes there is no alternative to killing people in the conduct of these operations. Such circumstances are extremely difficult for many people, including those who don't discover the difficulty until they've experienced years in law enforcement and hundreds of hours practicing combat skills on the range.

But there have been some new and highly effective training programs for police officers that have helped condition people to make good decisions about when and when not to shoot their weapons in potentially lethal situations—and to live comfortably with the consequences if they do kill a person.

Combat Shooting: Lessons of Gunsite Training Center

In northern, rural Arizona, outside the little town of Paulden, is an organization that has had a huge influence on all American law enforcement agencies, as well as the most accomplished of US military forces. It is Gunsite Training Center, Inc., now owned and operated by Richard Jee. Gunsite, formerly the American Pistol Institute founded by the legendary Jeff Cooper, has been tremendously influential because its doctrine is based on real-world problems and practical real-world solutions. Its programs are attended by Green Berets, SEALs, and SWAT team members from virtually every American jurisdiction, along with large numbers of private citizens.

Gunsite expanded on Coopers' fundamentals and developed a complete training program for using shotguns, rifles, carbines, special weapons, and pistols. The school is staffed by nineteen full-time instructors, twelve adjunct range masters, thirty part-time instructors, and thirty-five apprentice instructors. It has every conceivable kind of firing range for every kind of combat.

Despite its program diversity and large staff, Gunsite really has only one mission and one basic premise. The mission is to teach people to be able to participate in armed combat, prevail, and survive. The premise behind the mission is that success in combat is only partly based on marksmanship skills; it's mostly based on a particular mind-set and skilled gun

76

handling.

The training programs typically last five days, including one or two night shoots. More than a thousand students are accepted each year, of which roughly 60 percent are civilians, and the rest are military and law enforcement personnel. Since Gunsite's lessons have become almost universal SWAT team doctrine in the United States, the following is an abbreviated version of the lessons taught.

The Combat Triad

The essence of the Gunsite program is the "Combat Triad," a combination of mind-set, gun handling, and marksmanship. The Gunsite staff preach that a balanced combination of all three are required to win lethal confrontations.

Mind-set, the Gunsite instructors say, is the key to successful crisis management, a kind of mental conditioning that allows competence rather than chance to determine the winner of an engagement. It involves pre-planning and conditioning long before the engagement, and has been demonstrated over the years to be a strong factor in deciding who wins and who loses gunfights.

A major part of mind-set is awareness, a sensitivity to threats. Since armed combat is such an emotional, stressful situation, the Gunsite program teaches that anyone who carries a weapon must make a personal commitment to using it. While that might seem obvious, many law enforcement personnel have, over the years, failed to use their weapons when the time finally came—only to be killed themselves, or to see innocent civilians gunned down by criminals.

When an encounter begins, according to Gunsite, the attitude of the officer shouldn't be "Oh my God, I'm in a fight!" but "I thought this might happen, and I know what to do about it." Mind-set is important because, as Cooper learned by extensive interviews with officers involved in shootings, it is very easy for a skilled range shooter to fall apart and shoot wild on the street. Cooper's interviews reveal that many police officers, when confronted with an armed adversary and a shooting situation,

never use their pistol's sights, but instead point instinctively and jerk the trigger on firing their shots—with wild results. Gunsite instructors encourage students to evaluate their commitment to actually using their weapon to take human life. This kind of mental preparation is required, they say, before everything else. It permits the disciplined response necessary to successfully participate in armed combat with a handgun.

Gunsite students are taught to approach each potential combat situation with a measured level of awareness, from completely relaxed and unwary , (which they call "condition white"—in the locker room, for example, or at home with family); to the next level, an nonspecific alertness ("yellow"—while making a routine traffic stop, for example); to a specific alert ("orange;" expecting a fight—a confrontation with an armed, uncooperative person); to the trigger for armed combat ("red;" the suspect prepares to fire or has fired).

The Gunsite instructors teach students to convert their normal fear to natural fury.

The 9mm Israeli Uzi submachine gun was the first weapon of its type to be widely accepted by special operations teams. Note that the officer has provided a little armor for his elbows.

Here's another team at last cover and concealment waiting for the order to move up. They are armed *with MP-5s.* Heckler & Koch, Inc. USA/Steve Galloway

Anger helps the officer fight rather than flee, and helps focus effort and attention. Gunsite's classes teach officers to concentrate during the engagement on the technical business of accurate shooting. This extension of mind-set permits police officers to use the good marksmanship skills practiced on the range.

The Gunsite program teaches people to carry and use weapons in a way that combines officer safety and efficient use in combat. Gun

handling, as taught at Gunsite, conditions officers to be in complete control of their weapons at all times. Officers are taught to bring their weapons from a secure holster to proper sight alignment ("presentation" they call it) in about one second when a threat develops. They are taught how to clear a jammed gun under stress, and they are taught tactical manipulation (firing with the weak hand, from unconventional positions, or while wounded or injured).

Gun handling begins with proper carry in a tactical environment: for a single-action pistol, a cartridge should be in the chamber, the hammer cocked, the thumb safety engaged, and a full magazine seated in the well. This is "Condition One." Proper carry for double-action pistols is nearly identical except the hammer is down; this is "Condition Two." Both conditions permit the officer to quickly use the weapon while maintaining a practical level of safety. All police officers must learn to be in absolute and total control of their weapons at all times and in all situations.

Combat shooting technique is far different from shooting at bull's-eyes or plinking at beer cans. While that might seem obvious, millions of people have been sent into mortal combat with no better preparation than that (your author included). Combat is an extraordinarily emotional experience, win or lose. To win, you must hit the other guy before he hits you, and hit him with enough force to incapacitate him. As taught at Gunsite and all the other places police officers learn to fight, combat shooting technique includes three basic principles: accuracy, power, and speed.

Accuracy is the ability to place a shot precisely where you want—for a police officer, this generally means a dinner-plate-sized target at ten yards. Most people can achieve this easily.

Power refers to "stopping power," or the effect of the bullet when it strikes the human target. Stopping power is related to the caliber and cartridge; for instance, you will get radically different physiological effects when using either a BB gun or a .44 Magnum to shoot someone in the chest. Power is something you buy at the store.

Speed refers to personal reaction time—how long it takes you to fire your first bullet at your adversary from the time you perceived a lethal threat. According to Gunsite, you have about one second.

Accuracy without speed will get you killed; speed without accuracy will get you killed; and speed and accuracy without power may also get you killed. The three together are the essen-

Yooo hooo! Anybody home? The point-man is about to knock with a "flash-bang" stun grenade, a small explosive device that makes a lot of noise but doesn't cause permanent injuries. Heckler & Koch, Inc. USA/Steve Galloway

tials of practical combat pistol marksmanship.

Those are the *principals,* the theory of pistol combat; the Gunsite program uses them to develop the "Five Elements Of Technique": presentation, heavy-duty pistol, Weaver stance, flash sight picture, and compressed surprise break.

Presentation is the process of bringing the weapon from a secure carry position up to alignment on the adversary. The strong hand takes a firing grip on the weapon, and the support (weak) hand starts to move to meet the weapon in front of the body. Then the firing arm lifts the pistol straight out of the holster until the muzzle clears leather; the trigger finger stays out of the guard, alongside the frame, with the safety still on.

The heavy-duty pistol is the machine that

delivers incapacitating combat power, accurately and reliably, to the target; at Gunsite and in military, federal, and local law enforcement departments, the preference is for heavy (.40 and above) calibers, particularly the .45 ACP.

The Weaver stance is a two-handed, asymmetrical "fighting stance" using a push/pull grip that has proven to allow faster reaction to threats across a wide sector, better first-round accuracy and speed, and a faster, more accurate follow-up shot ("double tap"). This body position, along with the isometric tension it provides, controls the pistol during recoil.

"Flash" sight picture is an extremely fast sight-alignment technique based on *front sight* focus. Pistols, more than any other weapons, must be aimed rather than pointed, even at the typical short handgun engagement ranges. The Gunsite instructors stress this idea almost as much as range safety—maybe more—and it has been enthusiastically adopted by the SEALs and many other combat organizations.

The "compressed surprise break" is a technique for squeezing ("pressing," Gunsite calls it) the trigger to fire the weapon without jerking—a modification of the traditional technique, where the shooter squeezes slowly until the sear releases—but speeded up.

One of the most interesting and useful lessons officers learn at Gunsite programs is that winning a gunfight is nothing to feel bad about—despite what we read in the papers. Cooper's interviews reveal findings that contradict popular wisdom on how police officers feel after successfully engaging criminals in mortal combat. We've all been told how traumatic such a situation is for the officer, who—we are told—suffers great remorse over the incident.

A buddy team covers the back while their friends pop in via the front door. The weapon on the right is an MP-5 equipped with flashlight and a finger switch on the hand guard. This officer could easily "take out" one or more suspects in virtual silence. That silent-fire capability can be extremely valuable when multiple bad guys are engaged and hostages are in danger. Heckler & Koch, Inc. USA/Steve Galloway

Officer Rick Martinelli demonstrates the "guard" position with the MP-5SD. The weapon is mounted but carried with muzzle slightly lower for better visibility and less fatigue. He has identified his target, brought the trigger finger into the guard, and is bringing the weapon up to engage the target.

The truth turns out to be not only different, but to make a lot of sense: the officers who win mortal pistol combat with street punks, robbers, murderers, hostage takers, and all the other violent crooks, mostly report a kind of euphoria, relief, and satisfaction at being the winner instead of the loser. Cooper's teaching, continued by the new ownership at Gunsite, points out important distinctions between cops—who shoot genuinely bad, predatory people—and soldiers, who engage enemy soldiers who may well be honorable men; when a cop kills a crook in a gunfight it is *not* a tragedy.

Combat Physiology

One cop—who prefers to remain nameless, for understandable reasons—describes, below, how he made a series of potentially fatal errors during a chase that is typical of many officers' experience. The officer had been out of patrol for almost four years before going back on the

street. He and his partner got a call about a burglary in progress and responded to the scene. After getting a description of the suspect, they decided to cruise the neighborhood—and got lucky, in a way. After spotting the suspect, a chase ensued, and the officer pursued the suspect for a half-mile—over backyard fences, across streets, from one side of a residential neighborhood to the other, the hard way. In the process, every piece of equipment on his belt, except for his pistol, was lost: radio, flashlight, baton, mace, handcuffs. When the officer finally caught up with the man in a backyard and attempted to take him into custody, it didn't work very well.

"Boy," he says, "was I *stupid!* I must have jumped sixty fences! I got caught up in the chase. When I finally found him in the last backyard, he jumped up in front of me, and I was all over him like a cheap suit. I pushed him down, got my gun out, and—stupid, *stupid* me!—put the gun up against the side of his head. I commanded him to get down on the ground, but he is still trying to get away. Finally I was able to get my hand down to get him in a partial wrist lock, another stupid move, and I start to reholster my gun in order to have both hands free to put him in this control hold. So here I am with this guy, no way to communicate with anybody, no handcuffs, and this guy.

"As soon as he hears me put the gun away, he moves his hand down to his side, and when I grab him, I can feel something under his shirt; I thought it was a gun, but it was actually a big bowie knife. We struggled for a moment and I was able to throw him and then he was up again. We were about ten feet apart. I got my gun out again—and he produced a knife as big as a machete. I should have killed him right there . . . but I didn't. He started to move toward the fence again, and—another stupid move of mine—I followed him. But this time he swung that big knife at me, and I could actually feel the wind from it as it whooshed past my face. That was it; I popped him right then and there. He went down instantly."

As it turned out, the guy was on PCP, which accounted for his endurance. His "rap"

Engage! Officer Martinelli uses the Gunsite "flash" sight-picture technique to quickly align the sights on the target. The key to accurate combat shooting, with the submachine gun, pistol, rifle, or shotgun is front sight focus! With the front sight in clear focus, the rear sight will line up, and the target will absorb the round where intended. With a quiet little putt-putt, Officer Martinelli "double-taps" his target with two clean head shots. The Gunsite trigger technique is called the "compressed surprise break," a variation on traditional trigger manipulation. Shooters have always been taught to squeeze (or "press," as Gunsite calls it) the trigger until the sear disengages from the hammer, releasing the shot without changing the sight alignment. Target shooters do this with a slow, "open-ended surprise break" but Gunsite preaches an abbreviated version that happens much faster. The double tap, with any weapon, involves putting two separate, carefully aimed and fired shots into a target with maximum speed and precision. Although the weapon will fire thirty rounds in a few seconds, it is never used that way; in the Reno department, as elsewhere, a "zero miss" policy is in effect.

Most operators will carry the MP-5 if they can, and many like the double magazine assembly that H&K offers as an accessory. The MP-5 series of weapons are admired for their excellent fit and finish, as well as their design features and reliability—but they are expensive. This one has a sticker price of about $1,300—and you don't get to go pick one up at the local gun shop, either.

sheet went to almost thirty pages, with about fifteen arrests to each page. He had six prior escapes and eight assaults on police officers. He recovered and was sentenced to eleven years . . . to be released after *two*. Then he decided to make a career of raping old ladies right in the same neighborhood where he had been shot; the youngest of these was eighty-two, the oldest ninety-three. His next appearance in court got him 172 years, and he is expected to be in prison for quite a while.

In his SWAT classes, Dr. Ron Martinelli discusses "combat physiology," a set of physiological symptoms common to people participating in intense combat and experienced by the officer in the foot chase, a story Martinelli uses in his training programs.

"I developed tunnel vision," the officer in the previous incident recalls. "I lost my peripheral vision and my color vision—I saw everything in black and white. My hearing was sig-

nificantly degraded. I didn't hear the gun go off, although guys four blocks away heard it. The gun came up automatically, without my having to think about it. The sight picture came into alignment, I saw the gun recoil, the smoke, the impact, the guy go down . . . all in slow motion. When I remember the incident, I never see it in color or at normal speed. One of the things I learned from this is that you have *got* to be prepared to make the shoot/don't shoot decision."

Such situations happen to most officers, sooner or later. After one such foot chase and fight, Officer Ron Martinelli (he was a patrol officer at the time) had an attitude adjustment. As he explains it:

"That chase was an awakening for me; I was tired, I could taste blood in my mouth. I had just come out of a desk assignment, and was about eight pounds overweight, I was out of shape . . . and I made a promise to myself that day that this would never happen to me again. I went back into training and invented 'Martinelli's Law': The first objective of a law enforcement professional is to get home at night as unscathed as possible; the second is the thing we swear to do when we become police officers—to serve and protect. But you can't complete that mission without taking care of yourself first, preparing yourself physically and mentally."

Tools of the Trade

Choosing equipment for police special operations is literally a life-or-death decision for many officers, and every year the wrong decision is made by a few. SWAT team members look exotic and theatrical, for a reason, but there are times when the political forces that control police departments inadvertently put the lives of officers in danger.

For example, one city in California decided not to use the excellent and highly bullet-resistant Kevlar helmet—adopted by the US Army—because it cost too much, and perhaps because it looked too military. It would have probably protected one of this town's officers during a raid in which he was shot in the head; the officer survived, although he was critically injured.

Communications

Radio equipment for police use has to function reliably under the most challenging of circumstances. It has to let the officer communicate over the noise of explosions and gunfire, while wearing a gas mask, and after being banged around. It has to transmit clearly while people are whispering or screaming. It has to function all the time, without fail and it has to have a backup.

Police radios typically operate on the VHF (very high frequency) bands in the 150–174 KHz range. The hand-held models usually put out five watts and have a range of up to seven miles. While that might seem short, actually it is usually a lot less than that because of ob-

structions and the electronic interference often found in the urban environment. But such a short range isn't the handicap it appears, either, since most large towns and cities install many repeaters on the tops of buildings and on hilltops where the signal to and from units operating in the field can be relayed. The result is clear voice communication nearly anywhere in a jurisdiction. New radios for police applications use the 800MHz band and offer somewhat better security.

The radios tucked into the assault vests and attached to the equipment belts of SWAT team members are marvels of technological efficiency. They are sturdy, powerful, and simple to operate and maintain. Instead of the old, in-

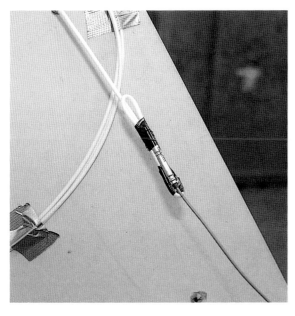

An electric blasting cap has been used to prime this coil of det cord, a quick and simple way to open doors, although not normally considered very polite by the folks on the other side. Such coils can be cut, assembled, and primed in advance of the actual entry; then, all you do is tape the coil to the suspect's door, retreat around the corner, and whisper, "Knock, knock . . . police . . . we have a warrant for your arrest" . . . then, BOOM!

Here's another application of explosives: these strips are small linear-shaped charges designed for opening those stubborn doors that resist more mild methods. With the concave side toward the door, the charge will cut through metal doors, hinges, and locks with ease.

dividual crystals that earlier-generation radios used, current-generation radios use a diode matrix and synthesizer that can program up to six frequencies from a single crystal. The result is much greater flexibility and reliability.

The built-in microphone and speaker is normally bypassed for SWAT operations in favor of a throat mike and earphone. While this is great for making it difficult for the bad guys to overhear you chatting back and forth outside the door, it doesn't make it impossible. In fact, well-funded crooks, particularly those in the drug wholesale trade, manage to buy scanners that cover the frequencies used by local jurisdictions, and sometimes invest a lot of time, money, and effort in working up lists of frequencies and callsigns used by the departments most likely to come tapping on the front door.

Body Armor

Most agencies have adopted the same Kevlar helmet used by the Army, and for good reason; it is comfortable, effective protection for the head. Shortly after the Army adopted the

Sgt. Steve Pitts inspects a test coil prior to Detective Carter's firing it. A normal coil of det cord for entry through a wooden door would be much larger and placed so that the resulting hole would allow the entry team to step inside easily.

design (and amid controversy about its resemblance to the old German model), one member of the 82d Airborne Division had a chance to field-test it during Operation Urgent Fury on the little island of Grenada. One of the defenders of the island scored a direct hit on the young man's helmet with a round from an AK-47 rifle; the soldier felt a hefty whack on the head, and then discovered the bullet sticking out of the Kevlar. There have been few complaints about the helmet since.

Almost everyone on an operation will wear some kind of body armor, and there are many kinds to choose from. The problem for most officers is to find a satisfactory compromise between mobility and comfort, and protection. Armor that is completely effective against .44 Magnum rounds or protects the extremities would make movement slow. It is a risky business, and calculated risks are taken. So most body armor covers the chest fairly well and is pretty flexible; it is hot if worn for long, but that's part of the compromise.

Eye Protection

Twenty percent of the injuries sustained in SWAT operations are to the eyes, so team members routinely wear full eye protection. These goggles have to be resistant to all sorts of impact, smoke, and fumes, and free of optical distortion; the ones used in police work typically use polycarbonate lenses.

Goggles aren't worn for all operations. They can be uncomfortable, particularly in hot weather or when a lot of running or heavy exertion is involved in the mission, so a lot of people avoid wearing them unless absolutely necessary.

Since things happen so quickly on a SWAT operation, access to equipment and its security are crucial. Team members wear combat vests based on models developed in Israel and the former Soviet Union, and by British military forces, and then later adopted by American Army Rangers. These vest systems are available in a variety of models from several commercial manufacturers. Each model has provisions for securely carrying radios, spare weapons magazines, handcuffs, and all the other items of equipment.

Blackhawk Vests

One of the best vest systems is custom-made to order by the Blackhawk Company in Virginia Beach, Virginia. The owner, Mike Noell, is a US Navy SEAL, and the designers and fabricators are all military special ops parachute riggers and police officers. Their motto is: By Operators, for Operators. A lot of their current customers are active duty SEALs, Green Berets, Marines, Air Force special operators, and SWAT team members from all kinds of jurisdictions—the FBI, DEA, and local police departments.

Besides vests, Blackhawk also builds other tactical equipment (including holsters, slings, bags, and cases for weapons and communications systems) to order—and just about no two orders are the same. Everybody has a different idea of where the spare magazines ought to go, where to place the pouches for the radio, handcuffs, and all the other items of personal equip-

A Smith & Wesson Model 5906. This is a common handgun on and off SWAT teams, one of a number of 9mm handguns that have generally replaced .38cal revolvers. The weapon has a magazine capacity of fourteen rounds.

ment. The foundation for each custom system is their V-1 Tactical Assault Vest, made from Raschel nylon mesh, on which pouches are attached according to the specification of the individual customer. Fasteners on this vest are a combination of Velcro and dot fasteners for security and ease of use. Blackhawk makes two basic types of vest, one for wear over bullet-resistant vests, the other for use without.

Vest design is an important subject for most operators because, in addition to providing quick and efficient access to essential items, the equipment in the vest can provide some measure of ballistic protection. Spare magazines, for example, can stop an assailant's bullet, so most SWAT operators try to use vest storage of the magazines as a little life insurance, as well as to ensure rapid access.

Ensuring the vest's contents are held securely in place is essential to the design. An officer must be able to run with one on—without pouches flopping around or things falling out. And the vest needs to be quiet; some materials squeak when rubbed together, and so it is important the contents not rattle or clatter when the wearer moves.

Holsters

Nylon has virtually replaced leather for all gun belts and holsters used in police special operations. Pistols are normally carried in a rig normally called a "dropped" holster, originally designed by the elite British SAS (probably the best hostage rescue team in the world), with the pistol carried low on the thigh and strapped to it to prevent flopping around. A couple of spare magazines are usually stowed on the outside of this dropped holster, with Velcro closures to permit rapid access.

Weapons

The fundamental tool of each member of a SWAT team is his or her personal weapons. All law enforcement personnel extensively study weapons and their proper use before they ever get to pin on a badge. Then, in most American departments, each officer must develop an extremely high level of proficiency with pistols,

shotguns, and sometimes with rifles. Many officers routinely fire 100 rounds a week, some much more. While there are many different ideas about which pistol or shoulder weapon is superior, there is general agreement that the only way you become a proficient combat shooter is by shooting. And most SWAT team members shoot so much they develop an intimate, intuitive knowledge of these tools that is sometimes amazing.

Of course, there are lots of choices among the pistols, rifles, shotguns, and submachine guns offered to law enforcement agencies: Glock, Smith & Wesson, Heckler & Koch (H&K), Colt, Ruger, Sig Sauer, and others. All have been proven by time, and each has its own set of devotees. Some of these weapons, though, have become particularly respected and coveted, and are profiled here. Both weapons and the kind and caliber of ammunition that feeds them are subject to endless debate and cycles of popularity. Currently, Glock and Sig Sauer are the generally favored pistols, the H&K MP-5 is the favored submachine gun, and .45 ACP is reclaiming the limelight as the favored pistol round.

Deciding which weapons to use on an operation, and what to feed them, introduces an element of art to the science and technology of special ops. Much depends on the expected engagement ranges, the combat environment, and the nature of the targets expected. One operator explains a bit about how you fit weapon and ammunition to a mission:

"In an op against a drug lab, you want to use a fully 'suppressed' weapon like the MP-5 with 147 subsonic ammunition, maybe Black Talon or Hydra-Shok ammunition. That's because most drug arrests take place in apartments, houses, or tenements, with drywall construction where even a hollow-point bullet will go right on through the wall like shit through a goose. The suppressor is important because it contains the muzzle flash and blast, reducing the possibility that you will ignite the flammable vapors so often present in these drug labs."

Drug lab operations also require extreme care about the most innocent of things—like turning light switches on or off. Even this action produces a small spark, enough sometimes to ignite the volatile chemicals that are often present.

The type of operation will influence the mix of weapons used. For drug raids, usually a combination of suppressed automatic weapons like the MP-5, plus riot shotguns, and semi-automatic pistols will be used. The shoulder-fired weapons will often have laser aiming devices and integral flashlights with grip switches.

Among police officers around the country, one sure way to start an argument is to claim that one handgun builder or handgun cartridge is superior to all others. Some adore the designs of Glock, others swear by Sig Sauer; one officer will tell you that nothing beats a .357 or .44 Magnum revolver, while another will claim that 9mm (or 10mm, or .40cal., or .45cal) is the best for the mission. In some ways they are all right: the best gun for you is the one with which you are comfortable and confident; the best caliber is the one with which you can hit your target.

Sig Sauer P220. This is one of the two or three most coveted, respected pistols available to people in special operations units in the military and law enforcement. It uses an aluminum alloy frame along with conventional steel components to reduce weight. It is extremely reliable, accurate, and easy to shoot in combat pistol scenarios. It is another European luxury model, with a price tag several hundred dollars above the sturdy Smith & Wesson.

Each caliber has its own set of virtues and vices. For example, the popular 9mm round is considered by lots of cops and combat pistol shooters to be a wimpy little thing that will almost bounce off someone. Some of that reputation comes from low-powered loads that were designed to keep bullets from "over-penetrating," or going through walls and striking unintended people after going through (or past) suspects. The popularity of "frangible" bullets that shatter on impact, preventing deep penetration, has added to this reputation, because on many occasions these bullets don't really penetrate the target, either. And it is true that people have absorbed numerous hits with 9mm rounds and still managed to keep fighting (assisted usually by large doses of PCP). So nobody claims the 9mm is the hardest hitting, best-stopping bullet on the block.

But, in its defense, the nine is compact, has a comfortable recoil, and you can stuff seventeen rounds into the magazines of some pistols chambered for the cartridge. Depending on the load, the 9mm can be a potent, lethal round; Federal's Hydra-Shok 9mm load with 147 grain bullet can whack somebody with about 350 foot-pounds of energy at a normal engagement range of about ten yards—a sure way to get a guy's attention.

Most jurisdictions have either a list of approved weapons and chamberings, or a list of criteria that each member of the department must comply with when he or she goes shopping for a side arm. Some, like my hometown department, limit magazine capacity to seven, although that is getting pretty restrictive. Others still require revolvers for the patrol division, with autos banned entirely. Some demand heavy calibers, like the .45 ACP round, while others require 9mm.

One sensible set of criteria for weapons is that of the South Carolina Law Enforcement Division (SCLED). Their criteria (as reported in *Shooting Times*, November 1990) state that weapons:
- Must be an automatic with double action on each round
- Must be suitable for all division assignments
- Must be 9mm (or, optionally, larger caliber) with 12-round minimum magazine capacity
- Must not to exceed 2.5 pounds loaded
- Must not have a magazine disconnect
- Must have rust/wear resistant finish
- Optional night sights available
- Optional compact version available

SCLED's requirements eliminated from consideration everything but the Smith & Wesson 5906, Sig Sauer P220, and Glock. A survey of the department members indicated that well over half wanted the new pistol to be chambered in either .45 ACP or 10mm rather than the 9mm, which had been dominant for the past few years. After extensive trials, the Glock was accepted in 9mm and .40cal versions.

Of course just about any round is potentially lethal; lots of people have been killed with .22cal rimfire cartridges, even .22cal shorts. One of the jurisdictions that has been helpful with this book reports four recent homicides resulting from one-shot stops with the diminutive .25cal automatic, a round that is not known for its stopping power. So it isn't just the caliber, or the load, or the bullet design, or the shot placement—it is all of these things together, matched to a particular tactical situation, that determines just which round is best. And, as Ron Martinelli says, "There is a lot of controversy and conversation about which is the best round and the best gun. My opinion is that the best gun is the one you can hit with, and the best round is the one you can knock your subject down with. The best place to hit is the place where you immediately incapacitate your target."

Det. Jon Buehler says, "The caliber is *never* as important as shot placement!" He should know, too, because as a homicide detective, Buehler gets to investigate all the shootings in his city, Modesto, California. Buehler is one of his department's firearms instructors and a competitive combat pistol shooter, and he has had to use his shooting skills against a human target in the most challenging pistol match of all.

A Glock 19. This Austrian "wonder nine" has found a happy home in the holsters of a huge proportion of American police officers—on SWAT teams and on the street. The Glock has a unique safety system and a stiff trigger that takes a little getting used to. The pistol created a sensation when it was introduced in 1983 because of its frame, an advanced polymer that some media weenies predicted would make airplane hijacking easier since it wasn't expected to show up on airport x-rays. Although there were calls for the weapon to be banned, it instead became incredibly popular with everybody who could afford it—except airplane hijackers.

"Although we joke about the 9mm round, we have had successful stops with it here in our department," Buehler says. "It's important to know that there is a difference between a fatal wound and an incapacitating wound. We now know that you can hit a guy in the chest, actu-ally take the heart out, and he still has fifteen to twenty seconds of oxygenated blood supply that can allow him to keep fighting. Just because you inflict a fatal wound on someone doesn't mean he is immediately incapacitated! The FBI guys killed in a shootout down in Mia-

Pistols are usually carried by operators in this type of "drop" holster. The design has been widely adopted by military and civil team members; the weapon is carried a bit lower on the leg than the conventional design, and the pistol's right where your hand naturally goes when your primary weapon fails to feed and there's a bad guy with an attitude problem around the corner.

Although displaced for years by smaller revolvers and then by the 9mm autos with bottomless magazines, the legendary Colt automatic pistol in .45 ACP chambering has been resurrected by many who use their pistols in combat. That's because there have been just too many cases where cops have made multiple hits on adversaries with the 9mm Parabellum round, only to have the guy stand up and continue fighting for a while. Two FBI agents were killed when a suspect who had been shot in the heart continued to fight and fire for many long seconds before he, too, died. The .45 ACP round has a far heavier punch, and after the FBI agents were killed, many officers started carrying pistols with the bigger round.

mi were shot by suspects that had taken fatal hits, but kept on shooting long enough to inflict fatal wounds on the agents. That incident has changed the way we all train.

"Somebody always seems to be coming along with what is supposed to be the 'miracle' round, but if you study them, they always have their own limitations. Some, like the Hydra-Shok, are good on soft tissue, but what if you have to shoot through dry wall, or a car door? In our department and on our team, we've reached the conclusion that the most reliable, all-around cartridge is the .45 ACP with ball ammunition. It has about 65 percent more frontal area than the 9mm. The ball version of the .45 is a reliable feeder, and it is a durable bullet if you have to shoot through windows, a car door, or a wall; it will stay intact a lot better than a hollow point will. The only advantage for the 9mm, from our perspective, is for the officer who doesn't shoot as much, and who will be less intimidated by the gun and the recoil. Some officers are more comfortable, too, with those extra rounds, perhaps because they aren't confident about their shooting ability."

Buehler, along with Sgt. Mike Zahr and Officers Dave Sundy and Vince Bizzini, teach the art and science of combat with pistols. Their program, like those of almost every other law enforcement department, is based on the lessons and doctrine developed at Jeff Cooper's Gunsite school in Arizona and promoted by the American Pistol Institute.

"Defending yourself in combat takes a lot more than just good shooting technique; you could take the best bull's-eye shooter in the country and put him up against a lethal threat, and he might fall all to pieces. Or you could take the guy who is as cool as a cucumber under stress, but can't handle a gun properly, and he might shoot all over the place and never hit his adversary. Good combat pistol technique involves a balance of speed plus accuracy—if you are too slow getting off that perfect shot, you'll get hit first, and if you shoot too fast and miss, the shot is also wasted. And, of course, you need the power of a good round when the shot is delivered," says Buehler.

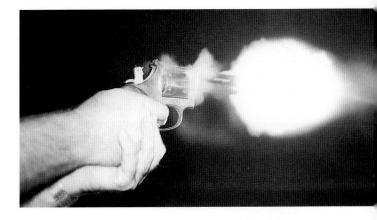

There are still plenty of big "wheel guns" around, but you won't find many on SWAT teams because of their limited capacity.

"You want to make sure that your actions are beyond reproach," Buehler says. "You have to avoid instigating the situation or provoking the subject. That means avoiding profanity and keeping your commands clear. You avoid provoking him, pushing him in a way that makes him feel he has to fight you to save face. We teach our guys that the options should always be the responsibility of the suspect, that what happens is his choice, dictated by his actions. We teach that you have to control your display of emotions, you need to appear calm and in control of yourself and the situation."

Buehler got to try out these techniques when confronted by a suspect with a knife during a 1989 incident. Earlier, the suspect had shot at his wife and, armed with a serrated kitchen knife, decided to take on the Modesto Police Department. "I drew my imaginary line that I was not going to let the guy cross, and remember mentally going through all my training. I remembered to control my language, to avoid profanity and confusing commands. It was 'Drop the knife! Drop the knife! Drop the knife!,' over and over. I felt confident about the situation—and, when the time came, I was able to make the shot. By following the training I got down in Arizona at Gunsite I had no guilt

A comparison of common auto pistol rounds (from left): 9mm, .40 S&W, 10mm, .45 ACP.

feelings afterwards, had no problems going to sleep at night. It was one of those things you have to do at work sometimes. Training was the key! If I had been put in that situation ten years ago there is no way I could have shot as straight or as confidently as I did, or that my actions would have been as clean as they were."

Glock

When the Austrian-manufactured Glock pistol hit the market back in 1983, its use of advanced plastics created a fair amount of media hysteria among people who feared that it would make aircraft hijacking even easier than it was already, since the pistol wouldn't look like a pistol on the airport x-ray security screens. There were calls for the gun to be banned, but the design survived and prospered in the marketplace, mainly among law enforce-

ment personnel who like it so well that many spend a lot of their own money to carry the weapon.

The Glock Model 17 is a lightweight, high-capacity 9mm handgun with a unique safety system. It is as homely as a mud fence but a delight to shoot—comfortable grip, smooth trigger (although it has a rather long take-up, and is fairly heavy), good sights, and mild recoil. It is easy to accurately "double-tap" a target, put-ting a second insurance round on top of the first. And seventeen rounds in the magazine! Police officers of the early 1980s, long accustomed to .38cal revolvers with only six rounds, thought they had died and gone to heaven. If you've ever tried to use speed loaders under pressure, stuffing six uncooperative bullets into six revolver chambers, then you are likely to really appreciate the life insurance represented by all that firepower—seven-

The Italian Benelli 12-gauge shotgun is pretty useless for shooting ducks, but it will help a team conduct negotiations with uncooperative citizens during operations. This model, one of several marketed to law en- forcement agencies, holds nine standard 12-gauge 00 buckshot rounds. Heckler & Koch, Inc. USA/Steve Galloway

teen rounds in the magazine for the Model 17, fifteen rounds of .40cal for the Model 15, fifteen 10mm in the Model 20, and thirteen in the .45 ACP Model 21. The Model 21 packs a heavy punch—in every way: it weighs over three pounds loaded.

But do law enforcement personnel really *need* all those bullets? A lot of departments said "no." Some still do and restrict magazine capacity to seven or eight rounds. Their feeling is that all those bullets just encourage people to bang away indiscriminately, and instead, those departments have what amounts to a "one shot, one kill" philosophy. The flip side of the argument says, "If we don't need those extra rounds, what are we carrying these speed-loaders around for?"

Glock has, along with Smith & Wesson, taken over a large chunk of the law enforcement pistol market, as one department after another has converted from revolvers in .38cal Special to autos in (usually) 9mm or .45 ACP. In fact (according to Glock anyway) over 40 percent of law enforcement personnel who carry autos are packing a Glock. Not bad for a company that's only been in the US market for ten years.

Sig Sauer

What's the most important specification for a combat pistol? It isn't magazine capacity, muzzle velocity, weight, or the stopping power of the cartridge—in fact, it isn't ever listed on the specification sheet. It is the reputation the weapon has among the people who've used it, the common belief that, when you pull the trigger the thing goes "bang" every time, no matter what. And, among the special operators in the Navy SEALs, the Army's Green Berets, and on SWAT teams everywhere, the Sig has a reputation for reliability that is unmatched by any other pistol. Given a choice, most of these people pack a Sig.

The Sig Sauer Model P220 is a double-action, nine-round, steel and aluminum weapon that comes in a variety of flavors: .38cal Super, 9mm Parabellum, and .45 ACP (seven-round capacity). The Model 226 is 9mm only, but has a fifteen-round capacity. All of them are *expensive*. You can buy other high-capacity 9mm autos for half or a third of what you'll pay for a Sig.

Heckler & Koch USP

Another alternative, and another example of German innovation, is the new H&K Model

USP (Universal Self-loading Pistol) in .40cal or 9mm. This handsome, beefy pistol is based on the same design that (in .45 ACP) has been adopted as the new "Offensive Handgun" by the US Special Operations Command (SO-COM), the umbrella headquarters group that oversees the Green Berets, SEALs, and Delta.

The USP follows the trend away from the 9mm toward heavier rounds in high-capacity automatics. Like the Glock, the USP uses a frame made of an advanced synthetic material, a fiberglass-filled polymer, instead of steel alloy for lighter weight. The magazine capacity is thirteen rounds in .40cal, fifteen for 9mm, but you can get extended magazines that accommodate twenty rounds for either weapon if you really need that much firepower. An interesting feature of the USP is that the frame is grooved

Fodder for the long guns. From left: .223 for the CAR-15, 12-guage for the riot gun, and .308 for the sniper rifle.

to accept brackets for laser pointers or an illuminator—both common additions to SWAT weapons that typically require somewhat makeshift clamps to secure to other pistols.

Smith & Wesson

Smith & Wesson has been the pistol manufacturer of choice for many departments who issue their force with the 3906 or 5906 models, both sturdy and dependable 9mm pistols with seven- and fourteen-round-capacity magazines, respectively.

The long, double-action trigger pull for that first round bothers some, but you get used to it. One police armorer says of the Smith, "It's a fine gun. All you need to do to smooth out the trigger is to put a thousand rounds through it." Not bad advice for smoothing out the shooter as well.

Combat Shotguns

When it comes to police shotguns, "old faithful" is the Remington 870 pump in 12 gauge, stuffed with five rounds of 00 (that's "double-ought") buckshot. Everybody agrees that when it comes to intimidation, the good old twelve, with its gaping muzzle and fearsome reputation, is just about tops. When most folks look into that big black hole, they generally become docile and cooperative—if they are sober enough to see it, anyway.

The shotgun is a close-quarters weapon, virtually useless beyond about twenty-five yards or so. That's because the shot spreads and slows rapidly, and the chances of hitting a man-sized target past that point tend to be nil, and the chances of a stray pellet or two hitting some bystander increase. A worst-case scenario occurred to San Jose's Police Department when one officer was killed by a stray pellet from another officer's shotgun during a shootout with a suspect who had just killed another officer.

But inside that limit, particularly inside of ten yards or so, the shotgun's output will be a lethal cone of fire that will range from a couple of inches across (near the muzzle) to a foot across (at ten yards). That pattern, a spray of twelve big lead pellets, is devastating when it hits; at close range it can punch a gaping hole right through a human torso or chop off a limb. The stopping power and shock effect are unbeatable compared to other weapons, with the possible exception of the submachine gun. When you hit a man center-of-mass with a shotgun, fired inside its normal effective range, it is like hitting him eleven times with a 9mm —all at once. Lots of people keep fighting after taking a single 9mm hit to the torso, but very few, including those blitzed on PCP, will fail to cooperate after a solid hit of "double ought."

The shotgun has many virtues besides simple stopping power. It points easily and is much easier to hit with than a pistol. It takes thousands of rounds of practice to turn a novice into a journeyman combat shooter with the pistol, but you can be on target and reasonably proficient in a hurry with the shotgun. That's one reason that the point-man on the assault team will be toting a slide-action 12-gauge, usually with a folding stock (or no stock at all), when it is time to drop in on somebody uninvited.

The weapon does have its vices. Since the shotgun is indiscriminate past twenty or thirty yards it is impossible to select a bad guy in any kind of crowd of hostages, the way you can with a pistol, rifle, or submachine gun, if you know your trade. It will put gaping holes right through walls, too, and sometimes—unintentionally—through people on the far side. And with only five shells in the magazine, you run out of ammo in a hurry, especially if the opposition includes multiple bad guys who decide to stand and fight. And although the folding stock (or no stock) versions are compact and lethal, they are extremely difficult to control for that second shot.

But there are things you can do with a shotgun that are virtually unique. One is that you can deal with an opponent in a fire fight who has taken refuge behind a car, for example, and is plinking at you with what he thinks is relative immunity. Nothing you've got will penetrate a car—but there *is* a way to make the guy rethink his tactical plan. If you fire a round or two at the pavement under the car, the shot will bounce and spray, with a high probability of hitting the guy in the ankle or calf. While

The CAR-15 with aftermarket lighting system. The CAR-15 combines some of the virtues of the submachine gun and the rifle.

these hits certainly aren't going to be fatal, and might not even incapacitate, they put a whole new tactical spin on the problem for the guy you're engaging—who will now probably be squirming around on the ground, using bad language, and repenting his sins.

Another virtue of the shotgun is that it will launch little CS tear gas rounds. Even though these are quite small, they can sometimes do the trick, if you can pop one through a window into a room where your suspect is trying to

9mm "ball" ammunition feeds reliably but doesn't produce a wound that is nearly as incapacitating as an equivalent .45 ACP ball round; hollow-point ammunition offers expansion at the cost of penetration. The .45 is, effectively, expanded when it leaves the gun. Everybody knows that even a 9mm hardball round will easily punch through auto body sheet metal—except that, in a tactical situation, that's not true. The lighter calibers bounced right off this trunk lid; inside the holes (sometimes on the other side of the car) are the .45 slugs.

avoid your advances. These "ferret" rounds will punch right through a wall, if necessary, before dispersing their perfume, but they require proper use to be effective. Normally that means you fire them through a wall, up toward the ceiling of the room so that the ferret round will bounce off and drop to the floor, rather than passing through a wall uselessly. Also, since the ferret rounds are so small, it takes several to be really effective—up to six or more for a single living room-sized space.

If all this wasn't enough, there are even specialized heavy slugs designed specifically for the 12 gauge for picking locks and removing hinges. The effect isn't very subtle (and it doesn't always work) but it can be quite effective on certain kinds of doors resistant to other entry techniques and tactics.

Remington 870

Remington has dominated the police shotgun market almost since gunpowder was invented. You'll find them in the racks of police cars everywhere because they'll take a licking

The Weaver stance has been adopted by nearly all combat pistol shooters. The stance allows quick engagements and rapid reaction to threats across the entire front, and provides a stable, secure firing platform. Proper technique, as preached by Gunsite and most contemporary combat pistol instructors, involves a push-pull grip, an asymmetric stance, and focus on the front sight instead of the target—followed by a smooth, rapid pressure on the trigger.

and keep on ticking. Some of these weapons are so old and decrepit that their wooden stocks look like they've been to war, but few actually get fired in combat. But the Remington 870 tolerates that kind of abuse, day in and day out, and still does what it is supposed to do: it fires when you pull the trigger, and it feeds the next shell without jamming when you operate the pump slide. Reliability and dependability, in weapons as well as people, count for almost everything in this business.

For that reason the 870 has been tradi-tionally selected over the Remington 1100, an even more popular shotgun with the sporting world, or other autoloaders. An autoloader *ought* to be the favored weapon for military and police work, but until recently they just haven't had the reliability required for life-or-death situations. But that seems to be changing.

Benelli M1 Super 90 Shotgun

Heckler & Koch recently started importing the Italian auto shotgun manufactured by

Benelli Armi of Italy. For a weapon that breaks with tradition, this shotgun made a lot of converts, as happened with the MP-5 submachine gun.

Unlike other shotguns that use propellant gasses or conventional recoil systems, the Benelli uses something called an "inertia locking" design. The system turned out to be more reliable than other designs and has been pur-

chased by many departments, even though the loading procedure is more complicated than that of conventional shotguns. Thanks to the design of the action, the weapon absorbs much of the recoil that punishes the shoulder of operators of pump guns. Not only does that action suck up the recoil, it converts it to a very high recycle time that allows a point-man to "double tap" a target almost as quickly as he can with a pistol or submachine gun.

The Super 90 series is available in several different models, but all are 12 gauge, three-inch magnums with chrome-plated barrels and chambers; barrel lengths range from fourteen inches to about twenty inches. The law enforcement models come with rifle-type sights, including the "ghost ring" rear aperture, protected by beefy lugs. In a recent test by *Fighting Firearms* magazine highly respected gun editor Peter Kokalis, reports that the gun fired a wide range of tactical loads with no stoppages at all, including the Federal Cartridge Company's special low-recoil law enforcement load of 00 copper-plated buckshot. This latter round has been somewhat notorious for producing stoppages in other autoloaders. Weapon capacities vary from seven to nine 2.75in shells, depending on model.

Other Shotguns

While Remington has long dominated the police shotgun field, they still have plenty of competition. Ithaca, Mossberg, Winchester, and others all sell excellent weapons to law enforcement agencies. Most of these are clones of John Browning's ancient and durable design for a pump shotgun, and most are chambered in 12 gauge.

There has been some recent interest, though, in 20-gauge shotguns for law enforcement, partly because of an increase in smaller recruits, male and female, who can't handle the bulk and recoil of a full-sized shotgun comfortably. The 20 gauge is a bit dainty but still can deliver twenty #3 buckshot, each about a quarter of an inch in diameter; even though the diameter is the same as that of a .25cal auto, the muzzle velocity of the shotgun round is twice as

Basic black is always in high fashion on the SWAT team, but leave the pearls at home. Two of Modesto's finest model the latest in proper attire for those special social occasions. Everybody seems to like having their vest set up and tricked out differently, and to accommodate them, a small industry has developed to supply assault vests to police and military clients.

fast. At close range this load will be deadly but have nowhere near the effect of a 12 gauge and its bigger "double-ought" buck. There have been reports of #3 buckshot being stopped by heavy clothing, although probably not within ten yards of the muzzle.

Mossberg sells one of these as the 500 Cruiser 20 gauge and has been promoting it to the police market; it has a barely legal barrel, 18.5in long and will accept standard and magnum shells. A similar version is offered by Ithaca as part of their Model 37 series.

A large after-market industry has developed to provide folding stocks, laser sighting systems, specialized ammunition, and other related products to customize sporting shotguns for law enforcement use. Also on the market are a few high-capacity shotguns that look more like Thompson machine guns than anything else, although they are used by relatively few departments. Others look like assault rifles with hormone problems, huge weapons of dubious utility. There are even a couple of shotguns available that are essentially 12-gauge pistols—with twelve-round chambers! These things must be almost uncontrollable, although the maker of one advertises that you can shoot twelve rounds in three seconds—but they don't tell you what you are going to hit.

Some departments forego the shotgun entirely in favor of small carbines in 9mm or other pistol cartridges, and Ruger is currently developing a weapon particularly for this market.

Submachine Guns and Full-Auto Rifles

About twenty years ago, submachine guns started becoming extremely popular with special operators in the military and law enforcement. That's when the Israeli Uzi started hiding under the jackets of the US Secret Service Presidential detail. The sub has some other virtues besides concealability; if you're any good with one, you can put the equivalent of a load of shotgun pellets in one guy—or even one part of one guy—instead of spreading the shot around on hostages, babies, and lawyers walk-

ing down the street three blocks away. In fact, the new little squirt guns combine the good features of the rifle, pistol, and shotgun when used within its fairly short range.

Uzi

The first of the submachine gun breed put into common use in the United States was the Uzi, a simple, reliable, proven—and heavy little

One of the things that goes in the vest is a radio. They get mounted in many places on the vest; this officer likes his on the left hip.

These little noisemakers are expensive! This one goes for about $30 a pop, and some (reloadable) go for even more. But they are helpful when it's time to drop in on the opposing team; you pull the pin, release the lever with your thumb, and chuck it in through a window. When it detonates, anyone in the room will be distracted unless they are already dead.

squirt gun. It comes in 9mm, normally with twenty-round magazines, and combines some of the virtues of the pistol (rapid fire, target selection, deep magazines, concealability), the combat shotgun (heavy weight of fire), and the rifle (utility against "area" as well as "point" targets).

Israeli combat experience with the weapon proved it could deliver lethal close-quarter firepower with a minimum of stoppages and breakage. American law enforcement agencies started buying them and using them on entry teams during special ops. It is a very compact weapon with the stock collapsed, easily carried in the open or concealed in a shoulder holster. The sights are massive—but you aren't going to have them break or bend in the excitement of the op as you might with other, more elegant, weapons.

Despite its virtues, the Uzi is a rather coarse and crude weapon. It looks like it was made from old beer cans and water pipe. It is clunky and heavy. The weapon is built almost entirely of steel sheet metal stampings, with a big steel bolt and a little steel barrel; high-tech

alloys and composite materials were never used on the old Uzi.

MP-5

The MP-5 is part of a large family of weapons that have become extremely popular with not just law enforcement but with the Army and Navy special ops communities, too. Green Berets, Delta, SEAL Team 6, the Secret Service, the FBI, and many other federal, state, and local agencies have all adopted the H&K line with great enthusiasm and have bought these weapons in large numbers.

It's easy to see why, too; all you have to do is pick up an MP-5—the fit and finish is superb, the balance is perfect, and the weapon comes up to your shoulder and points in a comfortable, natural way. Depending on the version, you can have a small, high-intensity flashlight up by the muzzle or a sound suppresser on the end of the barrel. With the selector switch on three-round burst and a full magazine, you can put rounds downrange in a business-like, efficient manner. Muzzle rise is negligible for the first two rounds, but the third will tend to go high until you learn to manage the piece.

With very little practice you can control the number of shots you fire without resorting to the three-round burst switch. The rate of fire is just slow enough for you to crank off one, two, five—however many you want. But the first two are likely to be the most accurate.

The MP-5SD has an integral sound suppresser that looks somewhat like a beer can stuck on the business end of the weapon. Shots from the MP-5SD are nearly inaudible when used with subsonic (low-velocity) ammunition. In fact, it seems that most of the sound generated by the suppressed MP-5 comes from the bolt face as it shoves a fresh round out of the magazine into the chamber—and the sound of the bullet as it impacts the target. The effect is really amazing, even to people who've fired a lot of suppressed weapons; all you hear is a very subtle *putt* from the weapon.

This feature is more important than it might appear. With suppressed weapons a SWAT team can remove subjects selectively, progressively, as the entry team makes a deliberate assault into a complex structure or location. The team can now take out one hostage taker without revealing to the others that anything is happening at all. And this isn't just a hypothetical scenario, either.

During the incident at the Good Guys store in Sacramento, the entry team from the Sacramento Sheriff's Office watched from hiding as two of the hostage takers escorted a female hostage to the bathroom. The team was thus offered the opportunity to take out half of the suspects but refrained from firing because of concerns about the consequences the apparent gun blasts would have on the fate of the hostages in the front portion of the building. That team, at that particular time and place, made the decision to wait, and as it turned out a lot of hostages were shot; but that's no criticism of them because they were the only ones "on the ground," and it might have been the best choice of the options then available. But that incident is used by other departments as a case study of a situation where the suppressed MP-5 could have offered one option for action that would not be available without a suppressed weapon.

There are lots of versions of the MP available, with different stocks, grips, trigger groups, and calibers. You can (if you have the proper ticket) obtain the weapon in 9mm, 10mm, and .40cal. One of the breed, the little MP-5K briefcase version is an executive model; it comes in a normal-looking brief case—but the handle is the trigger guard. You point the briefcase at the target, hope for the best, and squeeze the trigger; there is no sight picture, no Weaver stance. Without the briefcase, the little K model is only 13in long. This version is a favorite of many Green Berets and is called a "room broom." With it you can quickly and efficiently clean house as long as the ammunition holds out. The MP-5 Navy model offers single fire and full auto, without three-round burst; there are add-on suppressers for most models, but the MP-5SD3 is the d/ed leader of that pack.

CAR-15

The CAR-15 (Colt Automatic Rifle) is a popular little version of the M-16 used by the military for the last couple of decades. It fires the same little .223cal bullet and uses the same receiver and magazine as the M-16, but the CAR-15's stock collapses and the barrel has been severely trimmed. The weapon is available in several versions, including full-auto and three-shot-burst trigger group assemblies. While it is a good weapon, the CAR-15 is sensitive about what you feed it; I've seen one fail to feed repeatedly with otherwise excellent commercial ball ammunition, ammo that was feeding perfectly in the M-16s on the same firing line.

One police sniper I know tried to use a CAR-15 to take out a barricaded suspect who for hours, with his own rifle fire, held off cops from several jurisdictions. When my friend squeezed off his first round from his department's CAR-15 (he was called out without being able to collect his regular weapon) his first round scored a direct hit on the suspect's shirt pocket—only to have the highly frangible bullet shatter without penetration as it hit against a Timex watch in the suspect's pocket. Although the hit knocked the guy down and out, his wounds were minimal. The sniper visited the suspect later in jail and told him that he was one of the luckiest guys alive. And my friend doesn't let himself get talked into using other people's weapons anymore, either.

Night Vision Goggles

Night vision equipment is now readily commercially available to anybody who wants it and has the money. Stuff that was leading-edge technology and top secret just a few years ago can now be bought by mail order—by you or the drug dealer down the block—for a few hundred to a couple of thousand dollars.

Basically two kinds of technologies are involved: one that amplifies existing light ("starlight" scopes) and another—using thermal imaging systems—that works in total darkness and uses heat instead of light to build an image. Both systems have been adapted for several tactical applications, such as in remote viewing systems used in surveillance, goggles worn during entries, and weapon sighting systems. In addition to the viewing systems, many agencies use small, inconspicuous thermal beacons to identify people, vehicles, and locations; these little things are virtually invisible to the unaided eye but glow or flash brightly in the eyepiece of a thermal imaging system.

Thanks to night vision goggle (NVG) technology, police can observe and engage suspect behavior previously protected by the cloak of darkness. One cop describes how he and his partner used a set of borrowed military AN/PVS-7 goggles to intercept a drug deal:

"We had information that the Hell's Angels motorcycle gang was bringing a large quantity of dope into our jurisdiction at night, by boat.

Some jurisdictions keep all their call-out equipment in arms rooms and lockers within the department headquarters while others authorize team members to keep their gear in their cars. This department uses the former policy. In the racks are sniper rifles. Uzi 9mm submachine guns, shotguns, and CAR-15s— plus plenty of radios and flashlights.

We staked out the location from a distance and under cover. Sure enough, in the middle of the night we saw a speedboat approach the location about the same time that a big, black limousine drove up. The lights on the limo flashed, and the boat flashed its lights, too. The boat came into the dock and a bunch of biker types got out of the limo and started unloading something.

"We moved in on them, but with our car lights still off. They could hear us, but it was pitch black and they couldn't see a thing. But, since we had these NVGs, we could see perfectly what they were doing. We saw four guys get out of the limo, all with weapons, and they began to attempt to flank us. Then, what they heard from us was the racking of shotguns, and my order: 'Lay down on the ground! Now! Do it now!'

"One guy walked away, off the parking lot, with a gun, and hid behind a tree. I called, 'You—behind the tree with the gun—drop the gun and come out with your hands up!' He came out, but with the gun held low this time, and he finally dropped it. They never saw us, but we could see them almost as clearly as in daylight!"

Distraction Devices

There will usually be a few "flash-bang" devices in or on the assault vest of each member of an entry team. These little devices resemble a small hand grenade, and that's what they are. Instead of a spray of fragments, though, these devices produce a very loud noise, a very bright flash, and a fair amount of smoke. If one goes off nearby you are almost guaranteed to be distracted momentarily, and if the team's timing is good, you will be either shot or cuffed (or both) before you realize what happened. Despite all the noise, and despite the small quantity of mild explosives, distraction devices are quite safe; the container is strong enough that the explosion is contained and there is no fragmentation. It is possible to get a little burn from one if it goes off right next to you, but that is preferable to taking a bullet in the same spot, which is the normal alternative.

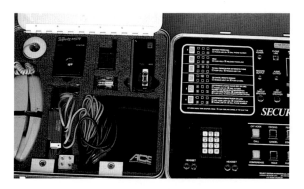

A secure telephone system, prepackaged for emergencies, is part of the SWAT team's kit.

Tear Gas

Tear gas is wonderful stuff—sometimes. When everything goes right, you get to bag your bad guy; he'll smell bad, and he'll probably barf a lot, but you will not have to put a hole in him to get his cooperation. In fact, you get to hang out on the street instead of going in and wading through his messy house—the guy will come out to you, and be almost glad to see you, too, if he can see you at all.

The problems with tear gas, though, sometimes make it completely ineffective, or worse. Some people can develop a resistance to it. Others are able to put together an improvised gas mask from things around the house. You can chuck a CS grenade or projectile through an open door or window, but a mild breeze can blow it right back out again before your barricaded suspect succumbs to its magic spell. Even under the best of circumstances, CS takes a few moments to take effect, a delay that can be fatal for the wrong people.

Another problem with CS is that the grenades generate a lot of heat, enough sometimes to set fire to the building. This is not usually considered good form, although it often produces the residents in short order. And if you have to go into a structure full of gas, you've got to operate while wearing a gas mask, a device guaranteed to limit your vision and mobility and ability to communicate clearly over the radio. So, while it sometimes works well, tear gas is a calculated risk that gets used only when its advantages outweigh its risks.

Surveillance Systems

A lot of the expense of setting up a SWAT team is the specialized surveillance equipment used—and there are a lot of choices for this type of equipment. Since the money to pay for the equipment often comes from drug asset seizures, there is often plenty to spend!

3-D Imaging Radar

Lately, a fascinating piece of equipment, which retails for about a quarter of a million dollars, is being promoted to SWAT teams: it's the 3-D imaging radar from General Dynamics, a modified military radar that actually lets you look into a building and watch what is going on

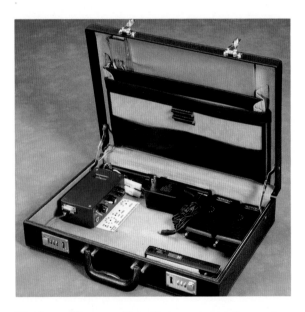

Hughes sells a small motion-sensing radar system that has interesting applications for SWAT teams. It can detect movement through brick walls and provide a warning to a surveillance team. It fits in a briefcase and goes anywhere—and only costs a couple of grand. Hughes/Advanced Electromagnetic Technologies

behind closed doors! The system uses a dual-band, millimeter-wave design (14GHz and 55GHz) that will work through glass, wood, drywall, and other common building materials. The military has used similar systems for years—with limited success—as battlefield surveillance devices to detect troop movement at night or in fog or rain, when other techniques don't work. This device lets you watch what is happening on the other side of a wall, look up through a floor or down through a roof. It is just the ticket for those hostage situations, drug deals, and barricaded suspects, as long as nobody's wearing a radar detector.

With the 3-D radar a SWAT team commander can know where people are in a building, and which ones are carrying weapons, and can watch the people move around and study the layout of the building's interior. It offers a new and unique ability to precisely study activity in places where suspects would normally think they were completely isolated and protected. At a quarter million dollars a copy, the 3-D radar isn't for all departments, but for big ones, with the budget and the mission to use it, the device could revolutionize the ways some situations are resolved.

Motion-sensing Radar

Hughes manufactures a handy little unit that will easily detect the movement of people through just about anything—including concrete blocks. The unit fits into an attaché case, is relatively inexpensive, and is sensitive enough to detect the motion of your hand. With several of these you can set up a perimeter around a barricaded subject and acquire a great deal of information about the subject without ever revealing yourself.

Spike Mikes

Bugging the bad guys has become something of an old, established art form. There are all sorts of sneaky little devices for eavesdropping on folks, and their capabilities are nothing short of amazing. They don't cost a quarter of a million bucks, either.

One company, Sam Mineroff Electronics

(SME), makes and sells a set of audio pickup devices that SWAT teams call "spike mikes." These are extremely small microphones on metal probes that can be inserted right through almost any kind of wall. All you have to do is drill a small hole (usually by hand, slowly, to keep things quiet) through the wall and insert the probe until the small tip is flush with the surface of the far side.

The probes are available from 2mm to 5mm in diameter, from 125mm to 400mm long. When attached to a microphone amplifier and an audio recorder, it is possible to covertly monitor and record any speech—and many kinds of activity—in one or more rooms.

In one operation a team installed one of these spike mikes into a room where a suspect was believed to be barricaded. After monitoring the room for a while, the surveillance specialist determined the suspect was not in the room because no activity could be heard; even if the suspect had been asleep, his breathing would have been audible. In another case, the specialist clearly heard a weapon being cleared inside a location being monitored, just the kind of information an entry team needs to know if they are planning an assault.

SME also sells an extremely small microphone that is only about a tenth of an inch square and can be hidden just about anywhere. The mike comes with a fifty-foot cable and can be used on a thousand-foot extension, with no loss of signal. If you have access to a room or location before your suspects show up, these mikes can be hidden under carpets or in many alternative locations. Then you can listen, with excellent clarity, to quiet conversations anywhere within a normal-sized room.

Pinhole Cameras

The same idea that produced the spike mike has also produced a remarkable kind of surveillance camera small enough to be inserted into walls. The camera system uses a special lens that has a front surface only a few millimeters in diameter. As with the spike mike, you have to drill a hole through the wall, something normally done carefully and by hand. The

Here's a dramatization of the motion-sensing radar; even though the guy in the hallway is tippy-toeing, trying to sneak up on the two guys in the conference room, the trusty radar beeps a warning. Now they'll have to stop talking about baseball until the boss leaves. Hughes/Advanced Electromagnetic Technologies

idea is to get a nice, clean hole on the far side of the wall that will not attract notice. Then a simple bracket is attached to the wall, and a support for a tiny television camera is positioned so the lens' front surface is flush with the wall on the far side.

The system works through the ceiling just as well as the wall. Together with a spike mike, the surveillance specialist can monitor and record any activity in the room, in real time, and share it with the team commander during planning.

Pinhole camera lenses come in many different makes, models, and sizes from about a quarter of an inch in diameter up to about a half-inch tube, each suitable for specific types of conditions. Optional accessories for the pinhole camera include infrared (IR) imaging tubes that "see" heat rather than visible light, and even IR illuminators to make it possible to view objects and activity in a completely dark room.

When it comes time to reach out and touch someone, call for the snipers. They can deliver the goods to within an inch at 100 meters. And while they are waiting for the chance to shoot, they will keep the CP informed with an accurate play-by-play commentary. Here, sniper Dave Kanter, police officer and Marine Corps Reserve captain, demonstrates his technique.

Chapter 4

Sniper/Observer Team

An officer selected for a sniper position on a SWAT team will already have some time on the force, will have been evaluated and tested in all the patrol basics, will have shown exceptional shooting skills, and—usually—will have expressed a strong interest in the team. Many snipers like to shoot and are hunters, on and off the job. A large portion compete in long-range rifle matches, usually sponsored by the NRA, the Army or Marine Corps.

New snipers may be able to shoot well, but that skill is only a tiny part of their team role. As snipers, they have to learn the team's approved techniques for camouflage, cover, and concealment. They have to learn how to select a position (a "hide") and to move into it, tactically, undetected. They have to learn to stay in position for hours, without fidgeting. They need to be nonsmokers and have good visual acuity and excellent memory skills.

"We generally want to be higher [in elevation] than the target, although that isn't always possible," one sniper says. "We want good escape routes—we need to have a way of getting in and out without being seen."

A sniper/observer team can be in position for many hours—ten or twelve is not unusual. Even with training and preparation, under the best of conditions, it is extremely difficult to stay in one place for that long. So snipers may be rotated in and out of position from time to time, to confer with the commander, use the bathroom, or to get a cup of coffee and stretch. For really long operations, fatigue becomes a factor and there may be a changing of the guard, with one SWAT team relieving another. Regardless, the sniper/observer position is always manned, and there is always some cover and concealment, and always a protected way for them to move in and out of the hide.

"Our team is not particularly high-tech," a sniper with a rural county sheriff's office says. "For example, I've trained with night vision devices in the Marines, but our county doesn't have any. I think you will find that most departments around the country may only have a couple of guys working as snipers, and they use their hunting rifles. And at its most basic level that's what it is all about—the ability to deliver long-range, accurate fire. It's nice to have the ghillie suits, the expensive radios and headsets, the telescopic sights, but you don't really have to have them to do the job.

"We tend to over-emphasize the high-tech equipment sometimes. I think we've even gotten hung up on the issue of accuracy of our rifles. Some people think we need sub minute-of-angle accuracy rifles that can put a bullet into tiny little spaces, when, really, if you can hit the head, that's good enough. Most rifles will shoot better than most snipers can. We need to get back to looking at the shooter instead of the rifle and the bullet combination."

There is a trade-off to concentrating solely on marksmanship, however. A sniper who is supremely confident in his equipment is more likely to be relaxed when it comes time to "pop a cap" on a suspect.

A sniper is normally paired with an observer who may be armed with a shotgun or other close-in weapon. Both will spend most of their time during a call-out studying their AOR.

Sniper/observer teams spend nearly all of their call-out time lying down on the job. If that sounds easy, try laying out in the sun sometime, wearing black, on concrete or asphalt, maintaining a constant vigil, and staying ready to take out an adversary the instant an opportunity arises.

Observer Skills

The primary job for most departments' sniper/observer teams is observing, rather than shooting. When the team is called out, the officers report to the TCP for briefing and assignments. Then each sniper/observer team will sneak into its assigned position, crawling if necessary, and will settle in to watch, wait, and report.

First, with unaided vision (sometimes called the "Mk 1 Eyeball"), you study the scene and take in the big picture. You look at the roads leading to the location, the proximity of the building to others in the vicinity, prominent features, and reference features (large trees, intersections, relationship to the CP).

Then you use your binoculars to start adding detail to the big picture: the location of the electrical box, the telephone cable entry point, the locations of all the doors and windows; is there a dog? A fence? All these details, and more, are identified by the sniper, and recorded by the observer on a sketch.

Finally, using a spotting scope or the rifle scope, you use the higher magnification to study critical features. How thick is the glass? What is the construction of the front door? Is there a screen door? Does the door open in or out? What kind of activity can be seen inside? What kind of furniture and other obstacles are visible through the windows? "The front door opens outward," the sniper reports to the observer, taking notes. "It has a deadbolt lock. The door appears to be made of wood, probably

111

Officer Lingerfelt sits in on the briefing with the rest of the team. He'll pay particular attention to the engagement policy issued for the incident. He may have the only opportunity to take out the suspect without casualties among the hostages, but the team commander will keep him on a tight leash until he feels it is time to call, "Green light!" authorizing the snipers to fire when able.

Although bolt-action rifles are predominant, the H&K PSG-1 is one of several automatics used by some departments. Bolt actions have an established record of shooting tighter groups than autos like the PSG—but, as many snipers point out, the weapon's accuracy isn't really relevant at the tactical engagement ranges for police snipers, which are normally under 100 meters. The other issue, the one that might even be more important than accuracy, is reliability; bolt actions almost never fail to feed, while autos have been known to jam.

hollow-core construction. The range is 140 meters to the front door." The license numbers of all the vehicles in the AO are reported and transmitted with the rest of the data to the incident commander.

All this information is usually transmitted to the CP via radio, preferably over a secure system and one with a voice-activated throat microphone. While larger departments have scramblers that make eavesdropping by the

This officer provides security for an observer. Both have taken cover behind a car about fifty meters from a post office where a barricaded suspect holds six hostages during a training exercise. The weapon is a CAR-15, a compact version of the M16 and a favorite of Green Berets and SEALs.

suspects almost impossible, most smaller departments in the United States rely on tactical channels that can be picked up by sophisticated scanners. Each sniper/observer team is likely to have its own channel to report back data to the CP.

A Marine Corps technique is used to train snipers to observe and remember things: ten unrelated objects are spread out on the ground. The sniper is given a few minutes to memorize the objects; then they are taken away, and each must be described. The drill is repeated, with progressively less time to observe the objects before they are taken away.

Another sniper memory drill requires the sniper/observer to take up a "hide" position on a range where many small, apparently inconsequential, items, such as an empty cartridge

Snipers slither into "hides" like this under the noses of bad guys, set up shop, and conduct business for hours without being detected. When the time comes, they can take out the suspect with a carefully placed shot that, if it scores correctly, will drop a suspect instantly.

case, a slip of paper, an old soda can, and a cigarette butt, have been placed. These objects are placed on tree limbs, peeking out from behind rocks, or are half buried. Each needs to be identified and sketched, and the range from the sniper/observer accurately estimated.

Novice sniper/observers must become proficient in the study of ballistics, including wind deflection, bullet drop, and the problems associated with shooting through glass. They learn how much wind at five, ten, fifteen, and twenty miles an hour affect the bullet, from the side or quartering; they learn how slant angle, high al-

Here's one way to show up at the party—a flight suit, flight gloves, and camouflage net head cover. This is a good setup for a hasty engagement.

titude, and temperature affect the flight of a bullet. "You really have to be on intimate terms with that rifle/bullet combination," a sniper says. "You need to know exactly where that bullet will hit every time."

"Obviously," one officer says, "we are looking for people who are extremely stable emotionally, people that can function well under stress. And for a sniper, this is even more critical. You may have to kill somebody in a rather cold-blooded way—the person may not even know they are about to be shot. It is a very different kind of problem than when you are on an entry team, where you rush into a building and confront somebody who has a gun and who may try to shoot at you. A sniper waits for a person to reveal himself, to show some sort of weakness, and then you take them out. It takes a

Dave Kanter's sniper kit. He's purchased it all himself, including the rifle in which he's invested a great deal of his own money. The Mini-14 is an observer's weapon, tricked out with a folding stock and scope. It is good enough to make a shot if necessary, but Kanter would much prefer to do his tactical shooting with the big bolt gun.

The CAR-15 is a common weapon for observers, sometimes employed by snipers.

Now, here's a sniper from the Santa Clara County, California, team with another German import, a sporty model also from H&K in 7.62mm.

Officer Lingerfelt has moved up to a position where he can talk to a suspect from a point of cover and some concealment. While the Remington 870 shotgun, even with rifle sights, won't permit precision shooting, it pretty well guarantees that the suspect won't be able to threaten the officer; the 12 gauge will reliably stop anyone at normal engagement ranges.

Officer Kanter demonstrates a hasty hide position. Using his rifle scope, he can closely observe his AOR; if the suspect appears and Kanter has firing authority, he can "pop a cap" on the crook almost instantly.

different mind-set from what is required of somebody on an entry team."

While the basic sniper class may last only a couple of weeks, and the specialized classes only a few days, training for most SWAT officers lasts as long as they are on the team. A new sniper/observer member of the team will begin the practical part of the training by working as the observer, rather than as the sniper.

Although much of the training and technology used by police snipers comes from a military background, there are tremendous differences between the two kinds of work. For example, the average shot fired by a military sniper will be at ranges of several hundred yards, perhaps over a half-mile. A SWAT sniper's shot will usually be at a target less than a hundred yards away; the average is about seventy yards.

Also, a military sniper normally doesn't worry about bystanders—but bystanders are a principal concern of the SWAT sniper, who must be far more selective about when and where to pull the trigger.

Green Light

The decision to direct a sniper shoot and probably kill a suspect typically will come from the team commander, although sometimes approval might have to come from a higher authority. Every team is a little different, but the consensus on the teams is that the decision is best made at the lowest possible level, preferably one level above the sniper. It is a perilous decision. One sniper explains:

"We always have, as police officers, the discretion to take immediate action to prevent loss of life. We can go ahead and act, absent a command to withhold our fire. There are some things that only the sniper can see through his

Kanter designed, built, and paid for his rifle himself. It is based on the Remington 700 action; a custom *barrel was added, along with a synthetic stock, adjustable butt plate, and a Harris bipod.*

118

optics. If, for example, we see the suspect threaten to stab someone, or actually stab a hostage, there just isn't time to call the CP on the radio and ask for a decision; there isn't time, and you have to act right away.

"But when you do that on your own, you take a lot of risk and liability if the decision turns out to be wrong. You can jeopardize other hostages, and there are other factors you might not be aware of. The commander has the big picture, and the sniper has the little picture he sees through the scope on his rifle."

The way it actually happens, though, is usually quite deliberate and well coordinated with the CP. The sniper teams will get a radio call communicating: "The entry team will assault in about a half hour; when you hear the 'go' command, you will not, under any circumstances, fire."

There will also be standing orders: "You are authorized to fire if necessary to save a life, or if the suspect comes out the front door with a weapon, you have the green light." Or, depending on the situation, the snipers may hear, "You will not fire, under any circumstances."

Sniper Rules of Engagement

In some departments, the sniper always has the option of "doing" the suspect anytime he or she thinks it is appropriate, just as the patrol officer is always authorized to use deadly force after certain criteria are established.

But special operations are different than bar fights and bank robberies, so some departments will put an absolute hold on the sniper during some phases of the operation. That's because there may be all sorts of things happening that the sniper can't see and can't be told about—like an assault team is already in the building and is about to take down the crooks, or all sorts of other situations that might only be made worse with a shot, even a perfect one. As one officer explains:

"Off duty or on duty, you have the right and the duty to use deadly force under conditions that are outlined in our operation manual—to defend your life, to defend someone else's life, to stop the actions of a suspect when those ac-

There is a lot of waiting in police work, particularly in special operations. This sniper, Brad Norman, Reno Police Department, waits for the other folks to get their act together. He, like most snipers, has taped a card to the stock with this weapon's ballistics as a reference.

tions would cause the public to be in danger. We can't shoot fleeing burglars anymore, but if some guy just shot somebody, and you can't stop him any other way, then you are authorized to stop him that way. So if you're a sniper, and in a situation where you could use your handgun at fifteen yards, you can still use your rifle to protect yourself or others from the ac-

Detail of the Harris bipod. This accessory is quite popular with snipers; it is light, strong, secure, and it works.

tions of a suspect. We are in this condition at all times, unless told otherwise."

Normally, a police officer has to see the suspect's actions in order to make the decision to shoot, but that's not the case in special operations. The team commander may know, from listening to discussions with the hostage negotiator, that the suspect will start killing hostages within the next few seconds—at the same time that the sniper merely sees the suspect chatting on the phone. Then, an explicit shoot order can be given by the commander to "cap" the suspect even though it might not appear necessary to the sniper. It doesn't happen often, and it requires communications and procedures that are perfectly understood by all— and that will hold up in court.

While being on an entry team requires a great deal of courage and commitment, so does being a team leader. Sometimes a leader's resolve fails during an operation, and errors of judgment get people killed unnecessarily. As an example, here is a case where the snipers had a chance to take out a suspect who had given ample cause for a green-light decision, but was al-

lowed to murder one person and endanger a whole entry element of a team.

"One of the worst cases we had in our department," one officer says, "involved a guy who had taken his girlfriend hostage at home. She was in a back bedroom, and he had threatened to kill her several times. All negotiations failed. He was armed. The snipers on the team had numerous clear shots at the guy—including one time when the guy came out on the front porch, by himself! The team leader refused to give a 'green light.' The suspect went back inside and killed the girl. Then he went back outside where he brandished his weapon at the point element of our SWAT team! *Still* no green light from the team leader! Finally, the point-man, armed with an MP-5, said 'F— this,' and killed the suspect."

There are several concerns that drive the sniper's decision to fire or not to fire at a suspect. Again, the commander of the operation may have information the sniper lacks, which might indicate the suspect must not be shot, in spite of the usual set of conditions that would seemingly authorize the shot. As one sniper explains,

"He could have a 'dead-man' switch on himself, connected to explosives; if he is shot and falls, the explosives go off automatically and kill all the hostages. Or there may be explosive vapors that could be ignited by the shot, or an assault team moving up behind the suspect, in the sniper's line of fire. The commander doesn't always have time to explain all this to you—he has to have a way to say, 'Do not shoot!' He just puts us in Condition 'Delta.' It takes the decision completely away from us."

The traditional authorization order to fire at the first opportunity (the second condition) will be a radio transmission that will say something like, "Sierra 2, green light!" The problem with that command, though, is that all the news reporters huddled around the radios in the patrol cars or the scanners in the TV vans can easily deduce what is about to happen— and will cheerfully go live on the air with a report that may sound like, "We're here at the CP where the shoot-to-kill order has just been given to the SWAT sniper teams!" If the crooks aren't too drunk or stupid, they will have a television or radio on, waiting for any such coverage, and now they know to keep out of sight. It is very common during operations against barricaded suspects for them to use the news media for their own intelligence data, and the media are normally quite willing to provide it.

"This kind of problem can be avoided by keeping the news media from compromising an op," one officer says. "And it is also why SWAT teams need to use 800MHz radio systems that aren't covered by civilian model scanners!"

Consequently, the teams work up more secure ways of transmitting the shoot order, including code words that won't make sense un-

less you're part of the plan. For one of these teams, the shoot order might sound more like, "Condition Delta is in effect," or any other predetermined word. The "don't shoot" order might be any other code word—"November," for example—but it must be well known to all the players. Just to make sure, some departments review the policy and the procedures every month and have everybody on the team sign off on the policy.

Sniper Rifles

Police snipers use a tremendous variety of shoulder weapons—stock or customized hunting rifles, often in .308cal chambering, or M-16s, CAR-15s, and even shotguns (but not for

A comparison of the .308cal and the .223cal cartridges. The smaller .223 is pumped up to quite a high velocity; it is accurate, but its bullet sometimes shatters rather than penetrates.

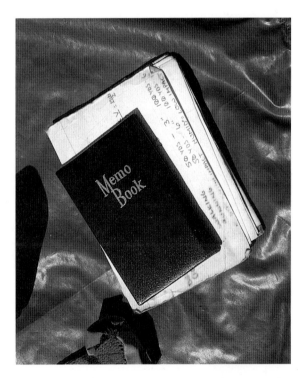

Snipers spend endless hours—and countless cartridges—developing firing data for their individual weapons. This data normally goes everywhere the gun does, helping the sniper plan each shot, no matter what the environmental or tactical conditions.

121

While one officer provides security, the observer develops a sketch of one exposure of a structure. The suspect inside appears occasionally, sometimes firing his big pistol toward any exposed officers or police vehicles, and screaming insults.

precision fire, of course). Most police agencies, and the civil government bodies they work for, are rather uncomfortable about using rifles of any kind, for any purpose. When high-velocity rifles are authorized, it is often with the requirement that special bullets designed to shatter on impact be used instead of the standard solid, copper-clad lead slug known as "ball" ammunition.

Concern about over-penetration will probably keep most police snipers from using one of the best tools of the trade for the military snipers, the .50cal rifle, which can reliably hit a man-sized target at distances up to a mile from the muzzle. The .50cal is stunningly accurate and has the power to penetrate car doors, plate glass, and almost anything else. The big .50cal bullet has so much retained energy, in fact, that it can easily punch a hole through the side of a car—and put a killing hole in the engine.

Such penetration power is the .50cal rifle's fatal flaw for most law enforcement applica-

After a dash across the parking lot, the sniper and observer move to within seventy-five meters of the building's back entrance.

tions, where the last thing the team commander wants is to have a bullet going through walls and striking innocent bystanders. Even so, the FBI has evaluated the .50cal because of its ability to shoot through the thick, laminated glass of airliner windscreens. On at least one occasion, a sniper has had a clear shot at a hijacker in an airplane cockpit, but the standard .308cal NATO cartridge used by most snipers (even with an armor-piercing bullet) was considered insufficient to assure a first-shot kill on the suspect.

While most police snipers prefer Remington 700s, a growing number are buying expensive German bolt actions and autos like the H&K PSG-1. But all tend to share the same basic features: stiff barrel, bolt action, synthetic stock, big scope, and big bullet. The market for these specialized weapons is sufficient that a lot of companies are offering elegant new sniper rifles aimed at the law enforcement market (and all the drug asset seizure money that has become available to fund this kind of acquisition).

One of these is the new Winchester Model 70 Custom Sharpshooter, a big, eleven-pound, bolt-action weapon in .308cal. The rifle is based on the tried and true Model 70 action mated with a heavy Schneider stainless steel barrel and inserted in a target-style stock. It is available with the excellent Harris bipod (the choice of most snipers everywhere, a sturdy, dependable piece of gear).

Observer Rifles

The observer's weapon is normally an "assault" type weapon, a CAR-15, Ruger Mini-14, or H&K 91, which is more suitable to the observer's secondary function of providing security for the sniper; the sniper's long rifle isn't really suitable for close encounters with the opposing team. The observer's choice of weapon has to be able to provide close-quarter, defensive fire and be accurate enough to deliver a long-range shot if the sniper is incapacitated somehow, or if the primary sniper weapon is disabled. For this reason, a military rifle, with a large magazine, good inherent accuracy, and

Sniper/observer teams may be armed with several types of weapons; they will establish an inner perimeter around the suspect, controlling all movement in or out, and reporting any activity.

suitability for both close combat and a deliberate, long-range shot is normally preferred.

The M-16 and CAR-15 are very popular. The M-14, with its bigger bullet and reputation for reliable accuracy, is also popular, as is the Ruger Mini-14 version chambered in .223cal. The Mini-14 is considered by some to be more reliable than the M-16, although the Mini-14 lacks the option of "select fire" (full-auto or three-shot-burst depending on model). "It's a fine observer weapon," a sniper says of the

Mini-14, "you could take a shot with it, if you had to."

The .223cal round has been a bit controversial in the law enforcement community, a product of its extreme velocity and perceived penetration potential. Horror stories circulated at one time about bullets going through multiple walls—and people. Recent tests have demonstrated about a 12in penetration in ballistic test materials—reasonable, many snipers say, for the job.

"A lot of departments will allow you to buy your own rifle," said Dave Kanter, "as long as it meets the department's criteria. In our case, that was a bolt action, .308cal, Remington 700. I submitted several proposals to get at least one semi-automatic weapon—the M1A was my first suggestion, which I offered to buy myself. That was denied. Then I suggested the PSG-1—the state-of-the-art sniper rifle—manufactured by Heckler & Koch and selling for about $8,000; I offered to buy it myself but that was shot down, too."

That department's reluctance to approve those weapons is based on legal liability concerns. When things go wrong on a SWAT operation, lawyers can be expected to execute operations of their own almost immediately, with huge costs possible. So department leadership normally tries to keep tight reins on such decisions.

Observers' weapons can be a plain-vanilla M-16 with iron sights, but variable power scopes are also common. Many observers' weapons are also equipped with folding stocks.

One Sniper's Weapon

Dave Kanter is a Marine Corps Reserve captain and a sniper for a sheriff's department SWAT team and has been thoroughly trained by both organizations. Rather than use the moldy old weapons his department offers its snipers, Dave built his own, at his own expense. "When you are talking about the possibility of taking a human life, where the possibility of just a tiny error can have disastrous consequences, I can't see going out there with anything less than the best."

The weapon Dave built is a .308cal chambered weapon, with a heavy "bull" barrel, on a model 700 Remington Police Special bolt action. The stock is a custom product made by the firm of H&S. The stock is made of synthetic materials and will accept the barreled action as a drop-in assembly with no further fitting. The stock precisely mates the barrel, the action, and the stock at critical points. The stock has an adjustable butt assembly, which can quickly be adapted to the shooter's needs and has a sturdy folding bipod to provide support for the fore end of the stock. The primary sight Dave installed is a 6–20x power Leupold scope, although he acknowledges that many snipers prefer fixed focal length optics.

"We had a burglar break into a gun store," said Kanter, "giving him access to lots of guns and ammunition. A patrol officer saw him break in, though, and sealed the place up, so we knew he was in there. Because of the situation, our team was activated and responded. We set up a perimeter, and my observer and I were placed on the roof of an adjacent building. In our department, the sniper team has a secondary mission to deploy chemical agents in a situation like this, so we had a lot of CS grenades.

"We got over onto the roof of the gun store and dropped a lot of CS into the place, then returned to our original position. Unfortunately, the gas didn't work—he had crawled up into the ceiling and pulled some clothing over his head. The entry team finally went in—and didn't find him at first. Then somebody noticed the ceiling, and they went up and got him."

Glossary

ACP Administrative Command Post, the part of the CP function that manages logistics, the press, communications, and related operational support. The ACP is one of two CPs, the other being the Tactical Command Post where the operation is planned, directed, and commanded. You get a cup of coffee and a doughnut at the ACP.

AO Area of Operations, the designated limits for individuals, teams, and the operation, defined during the planning process. It can be a whole shopping center or office building—or larger, the whole area affected by the operation.

AOR Area of Responsibility, the area within the AO that a two-officer team will have as a primary responsibility. For example, an entry team might have the right half of the living room of a residence as a primary AOR after the door-kick. A "sierra" or sniper team might have an AOR of the north wall of a structure, and if there are two sniper teams in the group, one may have the northeast wall, the other the northwest wall as AORs. A wolf pack (assault) team may have three sub-AORs within a building, taken in sequence after the door-kick. Individuals on the team will each have their own AORs within each room.

APV Armored Personnel Vehicle. Some teams use armored cars of the kind used by banks to transport cash.

"Avalanche" The code word one department has adopted to warn of possible explosives in the AO; it also functions as an evacuation order from the AOR. Other departments will use other words. If you hear, "Avalanche! Avalanche! Avalanche!" on the radio, that's your cue (in this particular department) to evacuate the AOR and dash back to the LCC for further instructions.

Breach To forcibly make entry, with a ram, a kick, or with explosives—through a door or window, or right through a wall if necessary.

C2 Command and Control, the process of controlling and directing an operation, based on military experience and principles of command in battle. The C2 in an operation is the operation commander, usually staffed by a person who is either the team leader, team commander, or the chief of police; the C2 is clearly identified in the pre-op briefing, and the C2 is, for the duration of the op, God.

CA Compromised Authority, when the crooks know you are coming—as happened at Waco forty-five minutes before the original assault that resulted in six agent deaths. When CA is discovered, one jurisdiction transmits over the tactical channel, "Jack rabbit! Jack rabbit! Jack rabbit!" Despite a careful plan for a deliberate entry and assault on a residence, if the subject comes out the door with a shotgun, one of the sniper/observer teams will probably make the CA code call over the radio to let C2 and the rest of the operation know there has been a sudden change of plan and the op will go down now.

CI Confidential Informant, a "spy" of one sort or another, often a relative or associate of the subjects. While "snitches" are frequently unreliable and often just as bad as the people on whom they report, the information they provide can save lives and is potentially very important.

Comm/Commo Communications, refers to the frequency or method (not necessarily radio, as comm can be through hand and arm signals, notes, or other code systems). "The comm frequency is 'blue,'" means the blue radio channel is primary for the op.

CQB Close Quarter Battle, the kind of combat that is a hallmark of police special ops, where engagements are at extremely short range and happen at extremely high speed.

CQS Close Quarter Shooting, the particular kind of engagements common to SWAT operations within buildings, with a mix of hostages and crooks, often in the dark, and with smoke and explosions nearby.

DAT/P Deliberate Assault Team/Plan, one way of moving in on the suspects, characterized by slow, precise, carefully controlled and co-ordinated movements; the alternative is an emergency assault team or plan, used when everything suddenly goes to hell.

Demo Demolitions, either the materials or the team members. Some teams have and use explosives to open doors, or to make doors in the middle of walls.

DVP Distinguished Visitor Protection, a mission often assigned to SWAT teams when the president or other famous persons come to town for a visit. Even a small team like Reno's has provided security for Presidents Reagan and Bush, General Schwartzkopf, visiting foreign heads of state, and public figures.

EAT or EAP Emergency Assault Team/Plan, used for hasty reactions to events requiring immediate action, such as the rescue of a team caught or overwhelmed during a deliberate assault. An emergency assault is conducted despite the plan for the deliberate assault, when there isn't a choice. These plans anticipate situations where a team member gets shot, or something else puts a crimp in the deliberate assault plan; the assault has to continue, using the EAT or EAP.

EMT Emergency Medical Technician, the team member or support staff who always is written into the plan to provide immediate aid to anybody who is injured during the course of an operation. An EMT on the team may very well shoot somebody, then immediately treat the wound he or she has just inflicted. The EMT is not normally on an assault or entry team, but may be part of an arrest team.

EOD Explosive Ordnance Disposal, the problem of getting rid of the case of old dynamite discovered in the basement of a residence or the det cord booby traps installed by a crook in a fortified house.

EP-1 or -2, -3 Entry Point One, a designated way for the entry team to go into a structure. It can be a door, window, or hole in the wall, which the demo team has just blown with a coil of det cord. Good teams normally brief at least two entry points, the second providing an alternative if the first doesn't work for whatever reason. EP-1 is normally the front door; EP-2 might be the front picture window.

Evac Evacuation team or plan. If hostages or innocents or wounded team members need to get pulled out of a residence, there is seldom time to sit around and talk about it; an evac team and plan will be part of the SOP and the briefing.

EXP Exit Point.

EX-1 Exit Point 1. The team will leave through a designated point in the structure, normally specified in the briefing.

FAP Final Assault Point.

HNT Hostage Negotiation Team.

INT Intelligence information, the detailed data needed to execute an operation. It can come from many sources—informants, pinhole cameras, and tiny microphones that can be inserted through walls.

Keep A secured location where people who have been pulled out of a location can be debriefed without distractions. The people kept at this location might be hostages or hostage takers who can provide information about who and what is still inside or still a threat to the officers conducting the operation. When a team has a distinguished visitor mission, a keep will be specified, perhaps by the Secret Service. Then, if something happens, a designated member of the team will take the VIP to the keep and will guard him or her, controlling access to the location, until a code word is transmitted indicating "all clear." Until then, nobody gets access to the keep.

LCC Last Cover and Concealment.

LP/OP Listening Post/Observation Post, the classic stake-out, surveillance situation where officers collect information without ever intending to make "hard" contact.

Medevac Medical support for the team.

MOE Method of Entry.

MOU Memorandum of Understanding, a formal (though not always written) set of instructions, guidelines and conditions for the roles of an individual, a two-officer team, or an entire special op unit. Essential for good team integration on an operation is to define the duties, responsibilities, and limits for each team member, particularly when people from different organizations participate on the same op.

NVG Night Vision Goggles.

Operator Member of a special ops team, a sworn officer participating in the tactical (not administrative) phase of the mission.

Op Plan A mission statement, normally written, that defines the operation's objectives and methods—a product of the team leader, team sergeant/supervisor. The op plan follows the classic five-paragraph order format used by the military.

Op Sec Operational Security, a set of procedures outlining how to avoid compromising the mission or its participants in any way.

Route When the subunits move up to the FAP, each will move along a designated route.

This is part of the briefing and will include possible "rally points."

Re-Org Another expression for the post-mission debriefing session, an evaluation of how the mission went, and how that compared to the way it was planned. A "lessons learned" session. Some teams do this quite formally, by subunits. The Re-Org is sometimes supported by careful documentation of the residence by officers who come through and make photographs and videotape records, maps, and diagrams of the location and its components.

ROE Rules of Engagement, part of the briefing and comes from the C2. Wolf pack ROE will be different than those for Sierra teams.

SCT Scout Teams. The scouts help find the routes into and out of the AO, into the FUP and the AOR. They also determine the construction of the AOR, its entry points, exterior door, and window construction.

Snake A common term for a six-officer raid team, moving in line; the first two officers are often designated the "point" element.

Shell A shell is often an invisible ring of officers around an AO; they may be observers on a surveillance team around a drug house or a half-dozen people in plain clothes around a distinguished visitor. One of the shell will be called a "shadow" man, an officer who will stick close to the VIP, and another officer will cover him or her, the whole shell providing mutual cover in a discreet way.

Sierra One department's term for a sniper/observer team, a two-officer element.

TCP Tactical Command Post, the location where the operation is launched and commanded, situated away from the ACP where the news media and crowds of curious bystanders usually congregate.

UC Undercover agent, a police officer acting under cover—as opposed to a CI, or confidential informant, who is perhaps a crook providing information for a payoff.

Wolf Pack One department's term for an assault team, a two-officer sub-unit.

Index